The Little Book of
PROSPERITY

Your Pocket Guide to
Wealth and Happiness

Maggy Whitehouse

A *Tree of Life* Book

Copyright © Maggy Whitehouse 2004, 2009

The moral right of the author has been asserted

All rights reserved.
No part of this publication may be reproduced, stored
in a retrieval system or transmitted, in any form or by
any means, without the prior permission in writing of
the publisher, nor be circulated in any form of binding
or cover other than that in which it is published and
without a similar condition including this condition
being imposed on the subsequent purchaser.

A CIP catalogue record for this book is available
from the British Library

ISBN: 978-1-905806-36-1

Printed and bound in the UK by DG3 London.
DG3 holds the environmental ISO14001
accreditation.

Tree of Life Publishing
Birmingham, UK

CONTENTS

INTRODUCTION

1. ABOUT THIS BOOK

The Little Book of Prosperity is an easy-to-read practical workbook on how to attract—and maintain—financial and emotional prosperity. A revised and updated version for the second decade of the new millennium seems a very good idea given the world's current belief in recession. As what we believe becomes reality, it seems that these are crunchier times for many.

First and foremost, it's important to say that how prosperous you are is completely and utterly up to you. It has *nothing* to do with any recession/credit crunch/financial meltdown that is being reported in the press or is being experienced by other people. External situations only affect us if we allow them to; we are the power in our life, not our parents, bosses, the media or our friends. The trouble is that we are trained from birth to believe that the world outside ourselves knows better than we do and we stop trusting our intuition. If we hand our power away we will get exactly what the others are getting. So don't be surprised or beat yourself up if you have been affected by the world's beliefs; that's entirely normal and human. The great thing is that you can turn that situation around *right now*.

It's also important to emphasise that prosperity is about much more than money. True prosperity is a state of mind where you are radiant with health, happiness, peace, joy and the knowledge that everything you want and need is yours for the asking. If you feel that, then you are totally prosperous whether or not you have money in your pocket. But feeling all those things is the key to financial prosperity, too, and there is nothing whatsoever wrong with wanting to be wealthy as well as whole. Apart from anything else, I know from personal experience just how hard it is to be spiritual, wise and wonderful when you are worrying about how to pay the rent.

It's a good thing to be happy and prosperous; happy, prosperous people are healthier and don't cause trouble in the world. So, rather than being selfish, you are doing everyone else *and* Planet Earth a favour by learning to create and maintain your own prosperity.

Many of us have a deep desire for abundance in our lives but often find it hard to work with money itself. However, money is the means of exchange that humanity uses every day and if we have a psychological or spiritual problem with money then that problem will have a knock-on effect on our lives in other areas too.

Why is that? Because money is purely energy. It is a means for exchange or barter and nothing else. As such it is no different from any other thought-form. However, over the centuries, humanity has projected so much negativity and fear onto money that it has become a kind of god, taking on attributes which were never intended.

People in holistic or spiritual work often have issues around money based on the idea that it is somehow wrong to be spiritual and rich or that their lives have to be all about giving to others and never receiving for themselves. Over more than fifteen years of teaching prosperity consciousness I have been amazed at how much resistance people can have to living an abundant life.

I once saw a woman *climb out of a window* to get away from a workshop because she was so upset by Louise Hay's prosperity video saying it was okay to be spiritual and wealthy.

Another time, I was asked to fill in at the last minute as a guest speaker for a self-development group. They had no idea who I was or what I did—and I didn't know anything about them either. I thought I'd test them out.

'This evening, I'm going to be talking about money,' I said.

'We don't want to know about that,' they replied, bristling. 'This is a *spiritual* group.'

'Prosperity,' I said.

'Oh, that's different,' they replied, brightening up.

No it isn't. And that is the whole point of this book.

Money was created in order to make things fair. Even more than that, it was invented to prevent dishonesty rather than to create it. Without money, there could never have been any trade.

Many centuries ago, one family had sheep and another had chickens; Family One needed eggs and Family Two needed meat, so they swapped. Then, one year, the sheep did not thrive and Family One did not have enough to share. However, they still needed eggs so they offered Family Two some kind of a token as a promise that next year they would give them two sheep instead of the usual one as long as they could still have the year's supply of eggs.

That token would have been exchanged in front of some independent witness, perhaps the village chief or shaman, so that the agreement had been seen to be made and no one could renege on it.

In the years that followed, the rest of the humans in that area invented a clever system whereby even if Family One were not able to honour their commitment to give two sheep that next year, Family Two could give the token to someone else for their sheep—and would be able to claim the originally promised sheep from Family One at another time suitable for everyone. This token came to be called money and it probably saved a lot of heartache and even lives. All it was (and is) was a physical representation of an honest agreement between people.

Because money is energy, how we run our lives financially is often a clear reflection of how we also run it emotionally and spiritually. However, people often feel a great resistance to the idea of working with money as a spiritual tool because of the emotions that we have been taught to project onto it.

In the prosperity workshops I have taught all over the world I have come across ten distinct areas of resistance around money. Each one represents a block which, when healed, has had a positive emotional, physical and spiritual effect as well as allowing financial abundance to flow.

They are:

♦ Emotional and mental issues with religion and/or God, leading to the fear that it is wrong to be spiritual and rich.

♦ Lack of understanding of how money really works.

♦ Lack of purpose or aim in life.

♦ Guilt and fear of being judged or resented by others for being wealthy.

♦ Forgetting to be happy and to acknowledge the abundance that we already have.

♦ Mental, emotional and physical clutter.

♦ Avoidance of monitoring or observing the

situation we are in. And to this I would now add 'running with an external situation because everyone else is.'

◆ Over or under-giving to ourselves and to others.

◆ Belief that there is never enough — leading to blocks in the ability to receive.

◆ Paralysis — inability to open the mind or to act in order to attract prosperity.

It is time to heal these wounds with money and allow it to be the neutral energy that it was always intended to be. After all, if we can learn to be prosperous ourselves, then we can teach others to do the same. That is, surely, a better answer to the problems of the lack, poverty and financial distress in the world than adding to them by living a life of fear, denial and discomfort ourselves. We can only help other people to release themselves from a financial recession if we lift ourselves out of it first.

Every suggestion, exercise and practical tip in this book has been tried and tested by me personally in a life of extraordinary ups and downs. You have to do the work yourself but even if you just do some of it, your life will become more abundant.

Does it work for me?

Yes.

Have I finished the work?

Heck, no! I'm still learning every day.

Is it hard work?

Sometimes, yes. It takes discipline. Later on, it gets easier (it's the opposite to a diet in that respect, thank God). The day you have truly cracked it is the day that you realise that you want to do this stuff for the rest of your life whether or not it works—because it is such a joy to live this way. That, of course, is the moment when you can't fail but to prosper.

There will still be days when you walk into negative energy fields, your astrology is challenging, you've got hormones or you are just too tired to be consciously aware of the good in your life; but they will become far fewer and it will always be easier to step out of them.

One of the reasons that I wanted to write about prosperity work is because I have made every mistake going, fallen flat on my face and 'failed' in several endeavours in the years that I have been researching and practising prosperity consciousness. But I have also been able to work out why things went 'wrong' or how it was just my perception which was trying to make them wrong because they were unexpected. In every situation, undesired events occurred only because I stopped doing the work or forgot to take care of myself. And, with remembering prosperity consciousness I have been able to re-build, amend and improve on everything in my life in ways that have amazed me. You can do it too and this book will help. Just remember to choose prosperity every day and with every breath. Enjoy!

2. FEELINGS AND EMOTIONS

The key to all of this book—and to all of prosperity consciousness—is to notice your feelings. Feelings are what the Abraham-Hicks teachings call 'your emotional guidance system.' If you feel good, then you are in alignment with your true self, your hopes and dreams and your destiny. If you feel bad, you are out of alignment.

It follows by the Law of Attraction that if you frequently feel bad, then you are going to attract more reasons to feel bad. And if you feel good, you are going to attract more reasons to feel good.

It is that simple.

The trouble is that we are such a confused mess nowadays about feelings! The majority of us have long been trained to tolerate a low level of unhappiness without even noticing it. I discovered this when I made myself take a week's Sabbatical while at home. I wanted to do a lot more meditation than I had been allowing myself to do and to read a couple of books which had been sitting, gathering dust on my 'to do' pile.

During that week I discovered my own level of low-grade chuntering where my mind chewed over so many seemingly-minor grievances and woes. Spending time in the silence of reading or attempting to meditate it was obvious that this groaning went on in my mind virtually all the time. And I didn't even notice it.

It explained a lot about my life; how I create wonderful things but every now and then I would have a downer that seemed inexplicable. It's entirely logical now I see that there has been a constant, un-noticed rumbling of discontent.

Interested, I asked some friends about their own levels of muttered grumblings. Every one monitored his or herself for a few days and came back saying 'yes, it's true!' We had been so programmed that we didn't notice it.

In addition to the grumblings that you may be carrying, there is also crisis addiction. This is just as dangerous as any other addiction and it is constantly fuelled by the media through the News, TV drama and soap operas. Something terrible must always happen any time someone's getting married or there's a happy occasion. Even good news must have a naysayer to grind it down to its 'proper' proportions. It has a lot to do with the belief that we must suffer for what we want so that we can be perceived to deserve it.

I fell into poverty consciousness at the same time as I got into holistic health. Having been a journalist on live radio and TV for 15 years and then experiencing marriage and widowhood within one year, I was a *bona fide* crisis addict. As the external influences of the news and a hectic lifestyle were no longer there, I had to create other sources of crisis.

When I married for the second time, I chose a man with his own brand of the same issue. He might be loving and spiritual in himself but his vibrational level, like mine, was a complete see-saw and we fed each other in those swings and roundabouts of crisis addiction. In his case it was issues with work and ex-wife and children and I picked up on all that energy and thought I was being supportive while in fact I was making myself feel dreadful. *And if I felt dreadful there was no possibility that I could be prosperous.* I simply didn't realise that and I sincerely apologise to all those to whom I taught mental prosperity consciousness for not understanding or explaining the importance of feelings. I did the best I could with the knowledge that I had at the time and I'm not beating myself up about it but, looking back, it's very, very clear that I was not allowing myself to be happy.

When my ex and I broke up (and there's a story of major crises involving three countries, eleven house moves and a beagle) I finally got the point and began working for real on creating a true prosperity consciousness.

Slowly but surely I learnt that it is one thing to learn theory and another to live it; one thing to be spiritual and another actually to be happy. And one thing to attract prosperity and another to allow it in. In the old days, it was fits and starts but now it's steady and sustaining. The difference is all in how I feel.

So, back to the Abraham-Hicks teachings. They

have a wonderful phrase which is: 'Nothing is more important than you feel good.'

Nothing is more important than you feel good. Wherever you can in life, do things that make you feel good. Even on the worst day, you can do *something* that makes you feel good even if only briefly. That's one of the prime reasons for visualisation: go somewhere in your mind where you feel good.

There is a difference between feelings and emotions. Feelings are transitory; you can feel bad one moment and good the next. You can cry at a sad movie and then laugh with a friend ten minutes later. Emotions are deeper-seated. They come from long training and they are usually the trouble-makers when it comes to prosperity consciousness. Negative emotions are the cause of the chuntering thoughts that create the low-grade unhappiness. They are such a deep and unacknowledged part of the psyche that unless they are triggered into full power by a crisis they are hardly noticeable. Eckhart Tolle, in his wonderful *The Power of Now* (Mobius), calls them 'the pain body.' Every time we give our attention to anything that we don't like the look of (someone's behaving in a way we disapprove of; the news is bad; there's a new rampaging sickness in the world) we feed this pain body and make it stronger. There are only two solutions: cold turkey from the News and soap operas and focusing on what we *do* want rather than what we don't want.

Heck, we give attention to the guy who's trying to beat us up for doing something which we thought was totally inoffensive, and we beat ourselves up far more effectively than he does! Its us that hurts us; not them. Generally, they only do it once and we repeat their action a thousand times.

It's the same with the word 'want'. Did your parents ever say to you, 'I want doesn't get'? The word 'want' is redolent with emotion for many of us. When we were very young we gloried in wanting things but we were taught again and again that wanting led to disappointment so we stopped daring to want and we learnt that it was selfish to want.

So, often, we scupper ourselves in prosperity consciousness by not recognising, when we set our goals or do our visualisations that we are feeling negative emotion around the word 'want.' To do an affirmation with a negative emotion hovering around is a worthless exercise. Worse, it's an exercise in bringing the opposite. So make sure that you find and use words that don't have negative contexts for you in order to feel good when you do any of your prosperity work (or should that be prosperity play?). My favourite affirmation for getting over that problem comes from Florence Scovel Shinn, the author of *The Game of Life and How to Play It* (Fowler):

'*My seemingly impossible good now comes to pass; the unexpected now happens to surprise and delight me.*'

That one gets round most emotional blocks.

You can never make the world a better place by focusing on the things about it that make you feel miserable. It's a long road to happiness and sometimes we have to walk it inch by inch but the secret to all of it is to seek joy in the moment. You can't get to joy on a road filled with misery so make sure that you constantly seek something pleasant whenever you can, whether it's cuddling an animal, smelling a flower or even having a cigarette. What *they* think is not important. What you *feel* is all-important. Just five minutes a day of uninterrupted happy thought will turn your life around. When was the last time you had a week when you experienced five minutes of uninterrupted happy thoughts every single day? You can do it; certainly nobody else can.

UNDERSTANDING MONEY

Money is a living energy. It needs to flow constantly, like the blood in our bodies, in order to bring life and health to its surroundings.

If it flows, it is healthy; if it is congested it is not.

A river rises as a stream in the hills, flows down to the sea and then evaporates. It falls as rain, raising the water table and rising again as the stream.

If the river is dammed by a beaver then, to start with, it creates a large abundant pool—but this apparent prosperity does not last. The water either builds up behind the dam and bursts it, flooding uncontrollably down the hillside, or it diverts to somewhere else, leaving a pool that becomes stagnant behind it.

Abundance is exactly the same. It needs to flow and it is amazing what kinds of things can stop it doing so. Thoughts, words, feelings, an overload of physical possessions—all kinds of things can block the natural abundance from flowing into your life.

This is a simple application of the Cosmic Law of Cause and Effect (also known as the Law of Attraction or Karma). This is emphasised again and again throughout most of the religious and spiritual teachings of the World in order to try and teach people how to run their lives to be wealthy and happy.

It's woven all through the Old Testament of the Bible but often misinterpreted because of the use of phrases such as 'the fear of the Lord is the beginning of wisdom' which implies that we must be afraid of the Divine Itself to understand life. However, the word 'Lord' in Judaic mysticism refers to the aspect of the

Holy One which is the Lawgiver—the creator of the Cosmic Law of Karma. Languages are funny things but the Hebrew usually translated as, 'the fear of the Lord is the beginning of wisdom' can be interpreted just as easily by reading 'respect for Cosmic Law is the beginning of wisdom.'

This aspect of the 'Lord' is also known as Shekhinah or 'the daughter of the Voice' and is referred to as the feminine or mother aspect of Divinity. In those days it was the mother who taught a child for its first seven years (the time it takes for the ego to form and belief systems to set) and, as most mothers know, the words 'no' and 'don't' are very important in those years in order to keep a child, fascinated by this brand new universe, from sticking his or her fingers onto a hot stove or into a piece of working machinery. So the Lord/Law was originally intended not to beat us up but to keep us safe from harming ourselves and others.

Cosmic Law—what goes around comes around; what you put out you get back; for every action there is an equal and opposite reaction—is the basis of the mathematical matrix on which this universe is designed. It is not judgmental; it is totally impartial. Cosmic Law reflects back what we have put out; kindness for kindness, love for love, thoughtlessness for thoughtlessness; generosity for generosity; laughter for laughter. When it refers, in the Old Testament, to 'an eye for an eye' it doesn't mean we, ourselves, have the right to take vengeance; it means that the Law itself will make everything fair, in perfect time.

Cosmic Law also repays us every thought and every word we think. By thinking of peace, joy and prosperity, we create just that. That's what it means when people say you 'make your own luck.' Fortunately, the Law works quite slowly and usually requires repeated

16

thoughts to create actions, so a one-off 'drop dead asshole!' shouldn't rebound too badly!

The Law of Karma is no different in essence from the Law of Electricity. We know that to make electricity obey us, we must obey it. You cannot make electricity work in any other way than the one that it does. Disobey it and it will bite—and even kill—you. It is totally impartial; it just is.

But if you obey the Law of Electricity, it will serve you. Electricity can be used to power engines, light cities, give heat and enhance life.

Money and prosperity work with this Law just as everything else does. So if you are not prosperous, you must be putting out messages of some kind that you do not want abundance in your life. This may be hard to hear but, if the Law is the truth, it must be so.

Whatever you say, think or believe about money reflects back to you. If you believe that there isn't enough, the Universe will hear you and ensure that your belief continues to be true. If you speak words of lack, the Universe will give you lack. If you constantly discount your work, the Universe will lower your income.

The good news is that this can be sorted—and you have the power in your life to do just that. The even better news is that if you change your words and actions, the Universe will respond to them even if it takes your thoughts and beliefs a little time to catch up. That is how affirmations work.

Never underestimate the power of words, even idle words. They are the most powerful tools in creation. How you speak about money affects what comes to you and what does not. The Universe takes things literally. The majority of catch-phrases which we use about money nowadays are negative. If we call money 'filthy lucre,' even as a joke, then the Universe is unlikely to assume that we think it is good or that we want it.

Some of the most common phrases that are used are:

Where there's muck there's brass
Rich Bitch
Blood money
Stinking rich
Money is the root of all evil
Poor little rich girl
For love nor money
Money doesn't grow on trees
Filthy lucre

STOP using these phrases. They will reinforce any negative feelings that you may have about money. If you can, try never to express a negative feeling about money again.

Similarly, when someone tells you that you look tired or you must be overworked—or comments on 'a vile day'— try not to agree with them. At worst be non-committal but, if you can, deny their belief either out loud or in your head. Just because they think it is a lousy day doesn't mean that you have to have a lousy day too. It may be a very good day but somewhat on the cold and wet side.

Does this sound over-simplistic? Try it out for yourself. You may be surprised how hard that is to do. Again, it's back to the feelings. You're either working your way up to feeling better or working your way down to feeling worse. And even if you get a moment's pleasure of agreeing with someone in their negativity, it will lead to another negative thought—and another and another. It has to, by the Law of Attraction. Nip it in the bud; think of your favourite thing/film star/food/ animal and turn your mind around.

Another important aspect in understanding your

relationship with money is identifying the loading you received from your parents. Were they prosperous? What is their attitude towards rich people? Did they ever refer to people 'getting above themselves?' Or, alternatively, are they prosperous and you want to rebel against them and their lifestyle to punish them? All these factors will have an effect on your prosperity.

Take a minute to remember your parents' favourite sayings about money. What's your absolute first memory about money? What was your childhood like? Did it teach you trust or fear? It really is worth taking the time to think back to find out how even the simplest of situations could have had a profound effect on you.

Here are some examples which show just how much and how long that first important impression can last. A childhood belief can have a profound effect on adult life.

Marie was always taught to put her toys away when her cousins came to play because her family were much better off than theirs. She was told not to 'show off' and, when she did have new clothes or toys that she could show to others, she learnt early to recognise the signs that other children disliked her for it and became more and more self-effacing.

Because of that, she was always shy of revealing how much pocket money she had or of being generous to others in case she was thought to be pushing herself forward.

When Marie began working she would never ask for a raise or promotion as she did not want to seem pushy or as if she was setting herself up as being better than others. She ended up marrying a man who was threatened by her abilities and she had to try even harder to hide her talents and not to outshine him. When she finally did dare to take a really good job her husband left her, so proving her inner conditioning and fear to be true.

When Marie came into prosperity work, she had a lot of inner conditioning to dissolve. She used the affirmations: '*I am the rich child of a loving father and I dare to prosper now*,' '*it is safe and good for me to prosper*' and '*I am willing to be prosperous no matter what other people think.*'

John had a piggy bank where he kept his pocket money as a child to save up for things that he really wanted. He counted the money regularly but, just as he knew he had enough to buy a computer game that he really wanted, he opened the money box to find that half of it had gone. Neither of his younger sisters would admit to taking it and his parents told him not to make a fuss.

He grew up mistrusting women—particularly over money—and could never make a commitment in a relationship because he thought he would be ripped off. He also made sure that he was in control wherever he could be and avoided situations where he was not.

He learnt to let go through breath-work and Shiatsu where he was able to let the practitioner move his body around while he relinquished control. He was also encouraged to seek for situations in his life—and in the news—where people had proved to be trustworthy and kind and to make a prosperity wheel (see Chapter 11) of images of people and situations that he trusted and which had helped him.

He also began talking to the people in his life about why he had become such a control freak and allowed them to demonstrate to him that they could be trusted—and that they understood his fears.

Susie's mother gave her a £5 note to buy some flowers for her grandma but when she got to the flower shop she had lost the money. Her mother was very angry and believed that she had spent it on sweets for herself. After that she would never trust herself with money and left bills unopened as long as possible—so 'proving' that she was bad with money and earning herself more 'punishment' through late payment penalties.

She had to learn to forgive and trust herself again and took a Louise Hay 'Love Yourself, Heal Your Life' workshop. She also asked a good friend to help her to monitor her dealings with money—checking her bank statement together and talking over money matters in a loving way which didn't threaten her.

She also gave her mother a gift of £5 just as a passing gesture and, in doing that, felt a huge weight fall from her. So much so that she was able to talk to her mother about the incident—only to find that it had been forgotten long ago. Her mother said she was sorry if she had over-reacted and that was a big thing for Susie!

Sarah wanted a scooter for her sixth birthday because the members of the 'in crowd' at school all had one. Her parents resisted because they said that she was too young but she begged and begged and, on her birthday, received just what she had asked for. She took it out on the pavement and fell over the kerb, breaking her arm.

She never willingly rode the scooter again. When she grew up, she still carried the belief that asking for something that you wanted was wrong and would bring pain—and that other people were more skilful than she was and knew better than her.

She began her prosperity work with the affirmation '*I love and approve of myself*' to help build her self-esteem and moved on to '*I trust myself and I dare to prosper.*' She also chose to spend more time with those friends who were not threatened by her prosperity and spent less time with people who spoke negative words and supported lack.

Of course, there are positive memories about money as well! But look for the patterns in your life to see what inner beliefs you have. These can be changed with conscious thought and working with affirmations. These serve to re-program your inner 'disk drive' so that you can change your attitudes.

Some good affirmations are:

♦ *I let go of worn out thoughts, worn out conditions, worn out relationships. Divine Order is now established and maintained in me and in my world.*

♦ *I am willing to be prosperous no matter what other people may think.*

♦ *I am willing to receive all the good and abundance the Universe has for me now.*

♦ *I open my mind to prosperity.*

♦ *What God has done to prosper others, He now does for me—and more.*

♦ *I give thanks for a quick and substantial increase in my financial income now.*

EXERCISE:

Test out the Law of Cause and Effect by being kind to strangers for a week; smile at people in the street, let people out in front of you in your car. Watch for how your actions return to you.

EXERCISE:

Work out what your parental loading may be by choosing one of the two following affirmations:

I am willing to be rich even if it makes my parents unhappy.
I am willing to be rich even if it means my parents were right.

MONEY, RELIGION, SPIRITUALITY AND GOD

It is perfectly good, reasonable, advisable and seriously okay to be spiritual and rich.

Those of us who were raised in or around the Christian religion seem to have the most issues around God and money. We may not have gone to church but many of the New Testament sayings, such as, '*It is easier for a camel to go through the eye of a needle, than for a rich man to enter into the kingdom of God*' and '*The love of money is the root of all evil*' are still embedded in our subconscious.

What we are traditionally taught about good and spiritual people also focuses on the idea that they were poor. We are told that Jesus was an itinerant preacher with no home; Buddha walked away from a life of riches; Gandhi lived in poverty; Mohammed lived in a cave; Mother Theresa lived with the poor in Calcutta.

One of the greatest weapons often used by those wishing to knock Islam is the 'proof' that Mohammed was not a holy man because of his wealth, merchant and warrior status and the fact that he married a rich older woman — and had a total of 22 wives and concubines during his life.

In contrast, Jesus is held up as a paragon of virtue due to his poverty. But, believe it or not, there is nothing in the New Testament that says that Jesus was poor. In Biblical days, the village carpenter was also a mason and one of the wealthiest people in town. The

Judaic tradition of the time was to welcome itinerant preachers into your home and feed, house and clothe them—and food was always left out by farmers for those who were passing by.

People also tend to forget that Jesus said a load of very positive things about abundance and prosperity, too, including the wonderful 'consider the lilies of the field' statement and 'ask and you shall receive.'

Jesus of Nazareth never lacked a thing—including the cash to pay his taxes. Had he needed money to pay a mortgage, the gas bill or transport costs, he would have manifested it with hardly a second thought.

The most often quoted New Testament objection to spiritual prosperity is attributed to St. Paul: 'The love of money is the root of all evil.' (1 Timothy: 6)

The 'evil' is the taking of the quotation out of context. This is what the King James Bible says:

Perverse disputings of men of corrupt minds and destitute of the truth supposing that gain is godliness. From such withdraw thyself.

But Godliness with contentment is great gain.

For we brought nothing into the world and it is certain we can carry nothing out.

And having food and raiment let us be therewith content.

But they that will be rich fall into temptation and a snare and many foolish and hurtful lusts which drown men in destruction and perdition.

For the love of money is the root of all evil; which while some coveted after, they have erred from the faith and pierced themselves through with many sorrows.

Here is my own translation (from *Novum Testamentum Gracae*, Eberhard Nestle, 23rd Edition:

Those with no correct form of living who defraud others can persuade themselves that wealth is their god. It's best not to associate with them.

However, to live in a perfect condition of alignment where no outside aid is needed is a great blessing.

We came in with nothing and we can't take anything with us when we go.

And having perfect sustenance and clothing let us be satisfied. For those who chase after money for its own sake need to prove themselves constantly and are prone towards judging life by wealth and possessions which is foolish and can lead to addiction.

For obsession with money is the basis of an unpleasant life and when some people have chased money they have lost their way in life and become deeply unhappy.

The Greek words for sustenance and clothing, *diatrophe* and *skepasma,* in ancient times covered food, housing without a mortgage or rent, four holidays a year (literally the ability to attend four religious festivals a year in Jerusalem), clothing, bedding, curtains, carpets (rugs), household equipment, all bills and taxes.

So, in a nutshell, it means:

'If we defraud others and we seek money for social kudos above and beyond having everything we need to live comfortably, we can lose our way and make ourselves unhappy.'

I don't think anybody would disagree with that!

What it doesn't say, but which is equally true, is that if we hate money or resent it, or spend so long sorting out our bills that we seem to have no time for anything else, we are still being avaricious—obsessed with the negative side of money. And feeling resentment at the riches of others is a sure fire way of harnessing the Law of Attraction to bring us poverty.

Certainly, Jesus was not a fan of cluttering yourself up with possessions. We all know the quotation, '*It is easier for a camel to pass through the eye of a needle than it is for a rich man to enter the Kingdom of God*' (Matt 19:24). This Kingdom of God, according to the Pharisaic oral tradition of the time, referred to an internal state of grace which was hard to attain when weighed down by the cares and maintenance of a lot of possessions. And of course, it also means 'you can't take it with you.'

One of the reasons why the Jewish people may have got so much flak over the centuries is because, as a nation, they are not afraid to be rich or to work with money. The Torah is a prosperity hand-book and the Old Testament Matriarchs and Patriarchs were rich cattle people, merchants, kings and queens. In Genesis 26:12 we are told that Isaac '*sowed in that land and in the same year reaped a hundredfold.*' At the time this happened, Isaac was living in a land where there was a general famine so his prosperity was not dependent on the condition of the general population. It's the same today. You don't need to be a part of anyone else's credit crunch.

Later, chapters 30 and 31 of Genesis tell how Jacob was able to build a prosperous flock from only the despised speckled sheep and goats given to him by his father-in-law Laban.

There are dozens of other Bible stories of prosperity and abundance. In fact the whole text, read consciously with knowledge of the beliefs and traditions of the times, is a prosperity workbook.

Buddha did turn away from life as a prince, having been over-protected as a child. But he tried the ascetic life of poverty and discovered that it didn't work at all. Both he and Jesus took 'the middle path,' leading lives of simple abundance without emphasis on possessions or attachment. That is one of the greatest secrets of prosperity—to allow it to flow to us and through us without needing to hold onto it or tie it down.

The message here, repeatedly, is that 'good people' want to live lives of balance and freedom without fear around where the next mouthful is coming from and with the ability to manifest anything that they need. That is true abundance—and it is our birthright.

Mother Theresa chose to live a life lacking in the comforts and possessions that most of us wish for but she was also a multi-million pound fund raiser for the Catholic Church whether she meant to be or not. There are those who say that she could have done even more good if she had been willing to embrace prosperity and use the medicines and scientific advances which were available for the people in her care instead of turning them away and choosing more traditional methods. She did what was right for her but she did not criticise other people's riches.

Gandhi's simple life came at a cost if his supporter, the Indian poet Sarojini Naidu, is to be believed. She said, 'If only Bapu knew the cost of setting him up in poverty!' Gandhi had an enormous entourage around him. Quite rightly; he needed it.

All the great spiritual teachers have had access to people who will fund them and take care of them—simply so that they can focus on the work that they need to do without distractions. They were supported by other people's wealth—by people like us.

If we want to become more prosperous it is worth considering how keeping ourselves in lack and poverty, through a belief that it is 'good' to do so, can possibly help any of the poor and needy in the world. How can you help the poor and starving if you are poor and starving yourself? It is those people who are sufficiently wealthy to give who can give the most help to those in need. Adding ourselves to the number of the world's poor is working against Spirit rather than moving towards it.

So, those of us who want to develop ourselves spiritually would do well to prosper financially, even if only to help those who inspire and guide us. That is the reason for the Old Testament practice of tithing. This idea of supporting priests and spiritual people has became distorted down the ages and tithing, instead of being something done voluntarily through love in return for inspiration, became compulsory so that churches and temples became rich while people were suffering. We'll talk more about that later in the chapter on Giving.

Religious teaching does have a lot to answer for when it comes to prosperity consciousness. There have been centuries of church and temple 'jam tomorrow' teachings of putting up with difficulties now in order to get to heaven later, which were just as much a way to control the masses as an attempt to encourage people to be good.

Corruption within religion hasn't helped and, for many centuries, Christianity has had a religious system that is loaded with wealth and giving out a strong message that God is rich, you are poor and that's exactly how He wants you to be. If you get rich, He will take it—or something else—away from you somehow as a punishment.

Sometimes we compromise and make a deal with God so that we can be financially secure but lack love in our lives. Or we have love but don't expect to have money as well.

It is possible to solve the issues around God, religion, spirituality and money as soon as you know that there is a problem and that it is affecting you. The first thing to do is to realise that you must investigate the truth for yourself. Don't accept second-hand opinions from anyone (even me!). Here are some hints to help you to start healing your relationship with God, religion and money:

♦ Separate out The Source from religion. Some of us call it God, others the Universe, others Spirit. Find the name with which you have the fewest issues and do what you can to understand what this energy force is.

♦ Understand that everything—absolutely everything – comes from this Great Source; life, light, vibration, love, money. It doesn't come from your parents, your partner or your boss; they are just channels of it and, if they aren't channelling what you want, the Source can easily find another channel for you—if you let It.

♦ Check out for yourself what is true and what is not. The Koran contains a very useful statement from Allah on these lines: '*You shall not accept any information, unless you verify it for yourself. I have given you the hearing, the eyesight, and the brain, and you are responsible for using them.*' 17:36.

♦ If you were born into the Christian faith check out what Jesus actually said over what the Apostles such as St. Paul said. The Apostles' teachings are often taken to be those of Jesus but they often differ quite radically. Jesus never recommended celibacy, for example, nor did he condemn homosexuality.

♦ Realise that the Law of Cause and Effect is

immutable, whether you believe in God or not. Our attitudes towards money and Divinity reflect back to us in our everyday life.

♦ Understand that all true spiritual teaching is aimed at reconnecting each of us to The Source in our own unique, individual way and that when we are aligned with The Source, we are able to receive Grace and abundance.

EXERCISES:

Find Biblical or other spiritual teachings within the religion of your birth which support the idea that prosperity is our birthright and repeat them to your self as often as you can.
Some useful examples:

'*Thou shalt remember the Lord thy God: for it is he that giveth thee power to get wealth.*' **Deuteronomy 8:17**

'*All things, whatsoever ye shall ask in prayer, believing, ye shall receive.*' **Matthew 21:18**

'*Ask, and it shall be given you; seek, and ye shall find; knock, and it shall be opened unto you. For every one that asketh receiveth; and he that seeketh findeth; and to him that knocketh it shall be opened.*' **Luke 11:9**

Allah promises you forgiveness from Himself and abundance. And Allah is ample-giving, all-Knowing. **Koran 2:268**

Shout at God! This is a very good way of getting

through sub-conscious fear and resistance around both money and God. Set up some kind of an altar—just lighting a candle will be fine—and have a good rant and rave at God for all the injustices you perceive in your life and the lack of financial security or abundance.

If this scares you then it shows that there is a deep issue in your soul about Divinity and this needs to be addressed. God will not strike you dead, damn you or be cross because you are angry. Instead, you may even sense delight or laughter that you are daring to stand up for yourself and seek your own path instead of believing what others have told you.

Write out the phrase 'I hate God because...' and fill in as many lines as you can. It will help you to clarify what you really feel (again, if you're worrying that you'll get in 'spiritual trouble' for doing this, it just proves the point!). Next, write out the phrase 'I would like God to be...' and fill that in too.

Write out the affirmation '*I am the rich child of a loving Father and I dare to prosper now.*' This is one of many affirmations that I use from Catherine Ponder, Unity Church's Diva of Prosperity Work—see her books in the Further Reading section. Put it up on the wall by the mirror in the bathroom and speak it to yourself every time you look in the mirror. Watch your reactions and if you can, make peace with them. Don't worry—the resistance will fade after a few days especially if you laugh when you realise that's all it is: resistance from an old emotional conditioning.

THE LITTLE BOOK OF PROSPERITY
PERSONAL NOTES & AFFIRMATIONS

OPENING YOUR MIND
TO PROSPERITY

A bundance comes from within. It is a state of mind which manifests in the physical world through our thoughts and emotions. It is important to put yourself into the flow so that you can start to reap what you truly want in life.

If you believe in a Higher Power, well then it's time to invest actively in the idea that God or the Universe is going to prosper you. The word 'inspire' means to 'breathe in' and if you want abundance you need to open up and breathe in the blessings that are yours.

If you are open to opportunities and lateral thinking there are all sorts of unusual ways that money and abundance can come to you.

Cutting God or the Universe out of the picture can be a serious block to prosperity because they play fair and if you won't look for, and accept, inspiration they won't give you any.

There is an old Jewish joke (but then, there usually is, thank goodness)... A man goes into the Synagogue and begins to implore God for money.

'I have wages to pay and a family to maintain,' he says. 'I need cash now! Oh Nameless One, let me win the Lottery!'

The next week the man is there again. 'Lord of Abraham!' he implores. 'My money troubles are getting worse. My staff are leaving; my business is suffering. Please let me win the lottery!'

And the weeks go past with the man renewing his

prayers all the time. Eventually, he is all but broken. 'Lord of Jacob, Lord of Isaac I must win the lottery! I must, I must or I am totally ruined.'

There is a rumble of thunder and a great voice echoes from the skies. 'My son,' says the Lord of Hosts somewhat wearily. 'Meet me half way. Buy a ticket!'

So often, we close the door on the thing that we really need because we don't think it through or open ourselves fully to the source of supply.

Not everyone is going to win the lottery—but everyone can listen to their own inner voice and to outer signs to show where they can open themselves up to prosperity.

One of the most important things we can do for ourselves is to work out just what it is that we truly want in life.

That may seem hopelessly simplistic but it's a step that people so often forget. They may talk about wanting a relationship or to be wealthy but, unless they make plans for the prosperity to arrive, all they are doing is focusing on the lack of it.

In workshops I sometimes ask people to write a two-paragraph obituary about themselves, as if they had just died. Then I ask them to write the obituary that they would like to have when they do die. The difference between the two can come as quite a shock.

From there, it's easier to see what needs to be done in order to live the life that they want to live, so that they can attract the prosperity that they want to have.

Aims are very important. Unless you have a definite plan for your life it will be hard to get anywhere. The odds are that you will end up living life by default. Even if your aim is one that some people might think ridiculous, you will get further by spending your life working towards it than you will without having any aim at all.

Do check out whether you are working towards your own aims, not the goals that you think you ought to want. Perhaps they are your partner's goals? Or the ones that your parents would like you to have? Or are they a legacy from school? Do you really know what you want? If not, then start making a list of what you don't want. It's a good way to start paring things down and clarifying. And guess what? How you really feel about those goals will tell you if you actually *do* want them or not. My ex has spent most of his life as an accountant because his family thought it was a suitable and impressive career for him. What he really wanted to do was work in the theatre. He appears to have made peace with being a financial advisor now but it was a long, hard struggle for him.

I wanted to be a novelist, so I became a journalist. I didn't realise that being trained to write in *précis* was hardly the best way to learn how to wax lyrical on descriptions and plots; I just did something I knew would earn me enough money and which wouldn't make my old head teacher laugh at me (which she had done when I said I wanted to be an author — there are those deep-seated but unacknowledged emotions again).

I did write three novels in the 1990s, all of which were published, but it was another decade before I wrote another one. I remember saying sadly to my friend Roger, 'I suppose I have to accept that I'll never write fiction again.' But Roger isn't the kind of man who lets me get away with statements like that and he spotted how I truly felt. He started brainstorming fiction ideas with me immediately and the following morning we sat down to breakfast and said simultaneously, 'The idea about the X-Factor and a modern-day messiah is brilliant!' That very day I started writing the novel and the joy in the writing of it was immense. My soul had known what I wanted—to write—but it took a real friend to help me identify the low-grade unhappiness I had created in myself by not believing that I would write fiction again.

We need long-term, medium-term and short-term aims. If you don't know where you want to go, it's hard to work out how you are going to get there. But once you know what you truly want to be, whether it's living happily in a long-term relationship, being successful or famous, being healthy, being an entrepreneur or a great cook—or all of them together—then you have a direction to help you to work out your life.

For example, your long-term aim or goal could be to set up your own business and help to heal other people. In that case, the short-term goal could be to research whether people actually want what you have to offer (a lot of people miss this step!) and find out if you need more training or experience. The medium-term goal could be to set yourself up in business, sorting out the finances and beginning the marketing that will attract clients to you. In spiritual work, this will normally include visualisation and continually working on yourself to become a beacon of light rather than trying to help others from a place of needing to be loved yourself.

Without that kind of planning, businesses rarely work. Neither do people's lives. Of course, some people do lead enchanted existences where everything falls into their lap and the world provides them with wealth for very little effort but I would venture to suggest that it is unlikely that those kinds of people will be reading this book!

They obviously carry a kind of prosperity consciousness in their very being to be so abundant and, when we've stopped feeling irritated about it, we can learn a lot from them and how they respond to life.

For the rest of us, who may have missed the boat somewhere along the way, there is comfort in knowing that prosperity work can turn your life around completely. If you can teach yourself truly to believe in the abundance of the Universe and your own link with it then you, too, can be as wealthy in all areas as the people who have achieved prosperity effortlessly.

If you do something every day towards your goals, no matter how small, then they will come towards you. They have to—the Law of Attraction is immutable.

Once we have an aim it is easier to work out what to do in our lives. Everything we do can be assessed according to whether it takes us towards our goal or away from it (and whether the prospect of doing it makes us feel happy or depressed). Of course, Sod's Law may offer some challenges on the way. I was once offered a wonderful chance to train for a specific job that I wanted at exactly the time that I had arranged to go away on a much-needed holiday. The next chance to do that training was nearly six months off and it was very tempting to cancel the trip.

But, inside, I knew that I desperately needed some time to relax after a bereavement and that I would not be able to operate on full strength for the rest of the year without a holiday. Ultimately, feeling rested and restored would do me more good in achieving my medium and long-term aims than jumping at the first chance offered to me.

And so it turned out... and in fact, that particular training would *not* have been the best one for me to take and a much better offer turned up within a couple of months, completely out of the blue.

LATERAL THINKING
Having an aim is very helpful when it comes to lateral thinking because it will encourage you to start looking

for ways towards your goal and to 'step out of the wave' to follow your chosen direction. People with prosperity consciousness are what Stuart Wilde calls 'fringe dwellers.' We don't follow the pack.

Fringe dwellers know that they are not limited to their wages; pack-people believe that they are.

The most prosperous people are very aware that money can come from all quarters and the more we can open our minds to prosperity, the easier it is for it to find us. Remember, money is an energy that responds to your thought vibrations. Think that it is limited and guess what? The Law of Attraction will demonstrate that to you. Think that it can come from anywhere and, guess what…?

If you limit your mind to believing that there are only certain sources that can prosper you, then you cut off other possible ways of being prospered.

Catherine Ponder has a great affirmation:

I do not depend on persons or conditions for my prosperity. I bless persons and conditions as channels of my prosperity but God is the source of my supply. God provides His own amazing channels of supply now.

That opens the door!

Money can come from anywhere—and so can love. Abundance can literally fall down from the skies. The secret is not to close off your options and to be open to absolutely everything that could come to you (and even things which would appear to be impossible).

Start informing the Universe that you are open to strange channels of supply. Affirm that you are opening your mind to prosperity. Pick up every penny you see in the street, keep your eyes open for good opportunities, always watch what you say and do to ensure that you are making sure that the Universe knows that you are open to wonderful surprises.

FOLLOW YOUR BLISS

The great American mystic, Joseph Campbell, said that the secret of life was to 'follow your bliss.'

If you truly do that, the Universe will return bliss to you. I get a horrifyingly large amount of clients who haven't got a clue what their bliss might be; it has never occurred to them to look for it, let alone accept that it might be possible.

Defining your aims will help you to find your bliss. If your aim doesn't make you feel good, then it isn't your bliss. Period.

Even so, you have to be pretty enlightened to be able to follow your bliss without a load of secret inner doubts and fears about whether you are worthy to be so happy, or those nasty little sayings that creep up now and again from the subconscious about things 'being too good to be true.'

Absolutely nothing is too good to be true—but we are all very capable of scuppering ourselves without knowing it. This can be through running old patterns, not doing our research properly or being too idealistic.

If you can find a little bliss in every single day you are already on the way to prosperity and, whatever your aim may be, you are working towards it by creating happiness in your life.

Here, just for the heck of it, are a few suggestions of bliss from a group of my friends:

Making love, giving and receiving kindness, travelling, having someone to smile at each day, walking a dog, riding a horse, dismantling and re-mantling cars, drinking wine in the bath, prayer, meditation, listening to music, writing, having a massage, watching a movie with friends, stroking a cat, a weekend away on impulse, singing, laughter, eating strawberries or chocolate cake (or both simultaneously), playing with children, gardening, scuba diving, giving and receiving flowers, dressing up to go out, going to weddings and christenings, eating ice-cream, picking blackberries, dancing, kissing in the rain (and the sun and the snow), eating out, drinking champagne etc.

Make a list of your own ideas of bliss—and commit to doing some of them! One a day to start with is fine and it doesn't matter how small it is either.

Note that most of the things that bring joy are mostly actions rather than things. Are you acting in a way that will bring you your bliss? It can be as simple as putting aromatherapy oil in your bath at night or watching a comedy show. Once the Universe knows that you actually like doing things that are blissful it will support you in creating more and more bliss.

THE IMPORTANCE OF TAKING THINGS SLOWLY!

It's time to own up here about one time that I thought I was following my bliss and fell flat on my face—or so it seemed at the time. However, even what appeared to be a disaster had wonderful long-term benefits so I can't call it a mistake and I don't regret it though it was fairly scary at the time.

My ex-husband and I had a dream to move to the Rocky Mountains of the USA. We gave up our lives and careers in England, sold everything and bought a business in Montana. The dream was to ride horses and live the good life.

It didn't work out in the way we wanted it to and we were back in the UK again within a year.

The dream did not have sufficient foundation to happen and I'm sure that it sowed the seeds for the end of our relationship.

So, what happened? I can only comment from my perspective but if you can learn from this cautionary tale, please do!

◆ We were enthusiastic about both the short and long-term aims but I didn't give any attention to the medium-term—and we hadn't done enough research. Moving to Montana was the immediate goal, running a café the intermediate goal and running spiritual holidays and workshops the long term goal.

◆ The visa we had applied for was solely in my husband's name (on the attorney's recommendation) so I wouldn't be allowed to work in the USA or earn money. I was worried about that aspect but, in the end, I ignored it.

◆ We didn't know how to run a café—and we had hated the one day when I did a try-out at a friend's restaurant before we left. It didn't register with me that this was *not* exactly following my bliss. I thought 'it will be different for me when we are out there—I'm a spiritual person.' Such spiritual pride definitely comes before a fall.

◆ We fell into the trap of listening to townsfolk in Montana who did not want change and kept the café as it was instead of re-furnishing the premises and changing the menu to suit us, not them. Therefore it never became the dream that we had planned.

◆ It never occurred to me that cooking 5,000 feet above sea-level would affect all the recipes I took over to the USA.

◆ I had just published my second book in the UK but, instead of capitalising on and promoting that, I turned my attention away from where I was achieving success because I was in a hurry to go to the USA. This may also have been an inner block that actually caused me to walk away from potential success.

That's probably enough to be going on with!

In a nutshell, running a café and living in a country where I couldn't earn my living was not my bliss but I couldn't see the wood for the trees and my aims got confused.

However, the year in Montana brought me some truly wonderful friends who supported and guided me, it ensured that one of my books became a teaching tool in a Unity Church in Montana, it enabled me to ride quarter horses across National Parks in the company of elk and eagles—and to have the adventure of a lifetime in bringing my dog home to England via Spain on Passports for Pets. Also, the village where I stayed in Spain became the destination for the first international conference that I ran three years later and without the whole Montana experience I would never have discovered it. I also wrote a novel about that time in Spain—so it's even tax-deductible!

On coming home, I had to find work and an old friend offered me a job in an internet company. Within six months I was an internet entrepreneur starting my own company and becoming a Chief Executive Officer; I learnt business skills I'd never dreamed of; got to work for the BBC World Service and even set up the BBC's holistic health and spirituality site. I could never have dreamt of doing anything like that.

Once my ex-husband had gone his own way, soon after we returned to the UK, I found a deep love with an old friend who is everything I need—but never realised that I didn't have. Last year, my 'new' husband, Peter and I, went back to Montana and had a *wonderful* holiday. I re-acquainted myself with this lovely area and its delightful people and it was an amazing experience to be somewhere where there had been so much trauma and be completely at peace with it. Peter loved it too which wasn't necessary but was a wonderful bonus. It was a perfect evening when he said, 'Yes, I can see why you wanted to move here. I'd like to come back and visit again.' And we will…

So I'm glad that it all happened; I'm glad that my ex has gone on to (hopefully) a better life and I wish him well. I'm glad that I had the guts to risk it all — especially now I know that I would do it differently now. The word 'entrepreneur' means 'risk taker' and I am still taking risks. Nowadays, I know much better which risks are good ones to take and which are not — and that comes through experience.

So don't despair if your life has had its share of disasters. The secret of opening your mind to prosperity is to look for the good, the new and the different. Take it easy to start with and practice risking things slowly! But do also remember that at the end of your life the regrets are generally for what you did NOT do rather than what you did do.

CHANGING THE ENERGY

We live in a world of bad news, soap operas, grumbling, gossip and TV celebrities. None of that is real but the more attention we give to it, the more destructive it becomes.

Yes, of course, we need to be notified if there is real danger around; but how often do you hear the media reporting how more than five billion people per day got through 24 hours without any crises whatsoever?

Most 'bad news,' such as the death of someone we love, is incredibly private and needs to be addressed in peace and comfort. So why do we avidly watch other people's distress? What are we creating by default when we do?

Negativity is catching.

So, to prosper, change the energy. Stop reading the paper and watching the news wherever possible; avoid soap operas full of angst and watch movies with happy endings. Choose how you want to live your life.

When I was just back from the USA I stopped to talk to a beggar to ask him about his financial situation. He had zilch. Whatever he had collected on that day was it. He had no debts and no rent or bills. Sometimes he slept in a hostel, sometimes he squatted, sometimes he slept out. It wasn't a good life but what I found interesting was that he actually had more money than I had. What I had was credit. I was more than £7,000 in debt—and if I had had a mortgage at that time I would have been more than £100,000 in debt. And yet, the beggar was asking me for money. I was the prosperous one when I didn't have a penny.

Prosperity is in your mind, your heart and your soul. Choose it consciously and poverty cannot choose you. Whatever the appearances seem to be, you are a blessed and abundant being. You can have it all—and be blissful as you do.

EXERCISE:

Work out what you would do with the following gifts:

£100
£1000
£10,000
£100,000
£500,000
£1,000,000
£1,000,000,000

This will stretch your mind and clarify what you would do with unlimited finances. It's a good idea to do the exercise every month to see how your desires change and then consolidate. It's an even better idea to check out where your comfort level stops—and to ponder why you think it would be wrong to be that wealthy. While the goal is to be totally prosperous, it's no good going too far over your comfort zone at this stage because you'll feel negative—and the Law of Attraction will stop the exercise working positively for you.

EXERCISE:

Use this affirmation every day for a week—and for the rest of your life if you like!

'I am open and receptive to all the good and abundance that God and the Universe have for me now!'

LEARNING TO RECEIVE

Receiving should be the easy bit shouldn't it? We all want prosperity so why on earth would we subconsciously refuse to receive it?

Have you ever had the experience of cake or chocolate or some other kind of treat being brought to the office or your home? There was enough for everyone and over and yet, by the time your turn arrived, it had all been eaten or broken or taken away.

There may be enough for others but it will run out by the time it reaches us… that's a deep belief that many of us carry. So much so that we often subconsciously refuse to receive so that we can believe that we are the ones are holding power and rejecting our abundance instead of being let down by God or others.

People who work with breath, such as Rebirthers or Transformational Breath therapists, believe that this belief is rooted as far back as our birth. In ancient days, a baby was born and found its way to its mother's breast where it learnt to suckle and breathe before the placenta was expelled from her body. The child had time to learn breathing for itself at the pace which suited it and it felt safe.

Nowadays, the umbilical cord is clamped as soon as the baby is born and its alternate oxygen supply is cut off immediately. This could well lead to feelings of panic and fear that there is not enough and that it is a struggle to breathe.

If that is the first experience of a baby coming into this world it will be a very powerful one and, unless it is addressed consciously, it will have a knock-on effect for the rest of its life.

Most of us only breathe deeply if we are exercising or smoking. The rest of the time we take short, shallow breaths still believing, without realising what we are doing, that that is all we can do.

Actually, there is enough. After all, we don't wake up each morning wondering if there will be enough air to get us through the day, do we? We don't worry that the sun will stop rising either. There is more than enough money, too—it's virtually the same as air in that respect. Apart from energetic prosperity, there is enough *printed* money in the world today for every single human being to be a millionaire. The only issue there is about money is the distribution of its physical form.

At any second, thousands—and even millions—of pounds, dollars, yen and euros are being faxed, emailed or telephoned straight through us in virtual reality. Energetically, all we really have to do is to put a hand out and say 'I'll have some of that too, thanks.'

If this immediately brings up the feeling that to take some of that money would mean robbing someone else, remember, this is energy we are talking about. There is enough and more for you without depleting anybody else at all. The printed money is not *all* the money. It is only a representation of prosperity. We can have the cash or the equivalent any time we are in balance with ourselves and the Universe—it is all our natural birthright.

At the time of updating this book hardly a news bulletin passes with some report about the 'credit crunch' and the financial problems that are alleged to be occurring. But the strange thing about this is that *there is no less money*. Nobody has just burnt it all or exploded the gold that our economy is meant to be based on. It's just that the movement patterns have changed. They have changed because of people's thoughts and emotions changing. A belief is just a thought that has been repeated so often that it has stuck. So by changing your thoughts about money (or anything) you can change your belief and, if you change your belief, you change the reality around you. For many of us, this is hard even to imagine doing because, somehow, the idea of the world being in lack fits better into our comfort zone. No one has enough now; not just us... This is *not* a helpful thought for you or for the world.

In today's culture we are not encouraged to receive, rather we are expected to feel that we have to earn the things which come to us. Even worse, we are trained to look after everyone else rather than ourselves. They, of course, have the same training and refuse to receive what we want to give them... Therefore, to be able to receive extra money, unexpected windfalls and beautiful gifts for no apparent reason can be a sad challenge for many of us.

The odds are that there will have been at least one time in your life when you turned away something because you did not believe that you deserved it—or, more likely, didn't even notice it. But every gift which is rejected sets up a resistance to other gifts that may come.

'Hang on a minute!' you may say. 'I can receive! I want to receive! Just watch me spend my lottery winnings!'

Well, *have* you won the lottery lately? *Are* you as prosperous as you want to be?

Take a look at your everyday attitudes.

♦ If someone gives you a compliment, what is your reaction? Do you say 'thank you' and smile, knowing that you deserve their good opinion, or do you side-step the remark and put it down?

51

♦ If they say they like your outfit, do you say: 'Oh this old thing!'

♦ If they say you look good, do you say you feel lousy?

♦ If they say they admire your work, do you make a face and say it was nothing?

The Universe hears everything you say and, if you won't want to receive compliments, it will assume that you won't want to receive anything else either.

Take a good look at how you receive physical gifts, too. Will you let someone buy you a cup of coffee at the office without insisting on giving them the money every time? Even more, will you let them get you a coffee—or are you always getting the coffee for everyone else? When someone gives you a present that you really like, do you ever say 'you shouldn't have!' Don't! Why shouldn't they have? They wanted to make you happy. They have that right.

It is also quite interesting to notice how we react when we are given something we do not like. Sometimes it is a good idea to distinguish between the gift and the object given—if you don't like or want the object you can still acknowledge the gift as a good thing and pass it on to someone else who will appreciate it.

Not to receive anything, whether it's a compliment or a gift, is to deny the person who gives it to you the opportunity of giving. That is really quite unkind. Why should you be the only one who always has the blessing of being the giver? To be a giver, someone has to receive. It's your turn! Show up and just say 'thanks!'

Also, to deny the truth of what they are saying is to deny them. You are effectively telling them that their opinion is valueless if they think you are good-looking and you tell them that you are not. It's their opinion! They have the right to have you respect it.

Incidentally, the phrase 'it is better to give than to receive' comes from a 14th century proverb based on the phrase '*it is more blessed to give than to receive*' from **Acts 20:35**. This is St Paul quoting Jesus. Except that Jesus never actually said it! It is also worth considering that the translation of the New Testament Greek word for 'blessed' is more accurately 'happy' so it means that we are happier giving than receiving, not necessarily more favoured or better people.

Many people take the phrase to mean that they shouldn't receive at all and spend a lot of energy and effort pushing gifts away, whatever form they may take. Consider how you feel when you have gone to a lot of trouble to find an ideal present for a friend or relative and they have difficulty in accepting it. Do you feel you want to go to any trouble for that person in the future or is it easier just to give them something simple and uninspiring—or even nothing at all—the next time?

Sometimes you need to give to yourself in order to be able to receive from others. Have you ever noticed that when you splash out and buy yourself some flowers or a treat, someone else gives you a similar gift? If not, then start buying yourself some gifts and see what happens. I once knew a girl who complained that her boyfriend never brought her flowers. She began to buy her own flowers instead because she loved them and wanted them and she let go of the problem in her mind. Of course, everyone started giving her flowers then— even the boyfriend sometimes!

At one particularly difficult phase of my life, when I was downright miserable and was having one heck of a challenge creating conditions for receiving good, a friend gave me a bottle of perfume called 'Joy.' I wore the fragrance constantly—not just for special occasions—and it did me so much good to know that I was surrounded by joy. Whenever anyone asked me what I was wearing, I could say, with all honesty, 'It's Joy' and they would laugh and often hug me and say 'That's great!'

Of course, you may think that the things that you are working on manifesting in your life are different from presents or gifts. You may want a job, a pay rise, a new relationship. However, your subconscious, the Universe and God will notice that you are practising receiving and therefore getting ready to accept what you desire into your life. If you cannot receive small pleasures or accept small gifts into your life, how could you possibly accept the large sum of money or the wonderful job?

God is the source of all supply but usually we receive our abundance through other people. If we want a new job then we have to deal with the people involved. If we have an idea we want to develop into a business and we want funding, we have to be prepared to accept the money from or through individual people who may have their own desires and agendas. It can be counterproductive at this stage to be fiercely independent and want to do everything on your own terms.

After all, you cannot see the wider picture and God can. As long as you are not compromising your integrity, be willing to receive from any source that the Universe shows you.

A good affirmation to use on this part of the process is: '*I am open and receptive to all the good and abundance of the Universe!*'

When you *are* receiving there are three possible levels:

♦ You receive exactly what you want and everything is perfect

♦ You receive what you thought you wanted but you're not really sure it is what you wanted after all.

♦ You don't receive what you want or you receive something else entirely.

The first outcome is wonderful, you thank God for it and then you can go on to decide on something else to manifest into your life and start the process all over again.

The second outcome is great too, although it may not feel like it. You've manifested something you asked for into your life and proved that the process works. There is nothing to stop you thanking God for this proof that the system works and then going on to redefine what you want and having another go!

There may also be nothing wrong with the third outcome although it can be rather irritating! It may be that you are not yet ready for what you've worked on or, indeed, that during the process your wants and needs have altered. Look again at your life and your desires. Either shift your focus slightly (just that can make all the difference) or choose something else to work on and see what happens.

Sometimes God knows better than we do. That wonderful job that we think we want could be like being in an avalanche, changing everything in our lives including our relationships with our friends and family; we may just not be ready for it. We may even have asked for something that would be positively harmful to us.

Alternatively, the prosperity may have reached our lives but in a form we have not yet recognised.

After one of my workshops, one of the participants contacted me to tell me that she had worked hard on prosperity consciousness for two weeks but no money had come into her life.

I asked her what else had happened since the workshop and she said, 'Well it's funny; my neighbour was going on holiday last week and the night before she went her freezer broke down. She gave me all the contents to use because otherwise they would be ruined. Oh and my mother said she would pay for me to go on holiday to Berlin with her!'

Although she had not recognised them as manifestations of prosperity she had accepted them both, whereas she might have found it difficult to accept the monetary value of the freezer contents from her neighbour instead. She may also have felt that she would be company for her mother on holiday and the additional cost over the single person supplement was trivial, therefore acceptable. This woman had a lot more work to do on receiving but the Universe was doing what it could to show her that the work she was doing was effective.

It is as easy to manifest a diamond tiara as a penny but you may find it much easier to receive a penny into your life than a tiara. That's why practicing receiving is important. Notice what you do receive and be prepared to redefine what you want all the time.

EXERCISE:

Give yourself a treat every day for a week, whether it's flowers, chocolate, free time or a magazine. Note the resistance!

EXERCISE:

Ask someone to give you something every day for a fortnight. It doesn't have to be anything expensive—a flower from the garden or a compliment is sufficient. Your task is to accept each gift simply, however much or little it cost.

EXERCISE:

When anyone gives you a compliment, just say 'thank you' without denying it or giving a compliment back in return.

EXERCISE:

Pick up any coins you find in the street. That way you show the Universe that you are willing to receive money. If you only find coppers, start asking for silver. A woman who came on a workshop did that before the lunch break and found two 50p coins at lunch!

GRATITUDE

It was Abraham Lincoln who said that we can choose to be happy. That's quite a scary concept for people who are depressed or are going through bad experiences. If there is a serious problem in your life, then you may well need outside help in the form of support, counselling, allopathic or complementary medicine but even so, using your will to focus on goodness rather than badness whenever you can will contribute to the healing process.

For those of us who just want life to be better, being grateful for what we already have is a very powerful way of applying Universal Law—even if the idea of it does make you wince because your Grandma was always saying, 'Count your blessings, dear!'

Firstly, it shows the Universe that you are focusing your mind on the kind of things you truly want as opposed to concentrating on the things that you *don't* want. Secondly, it helps you remember yourself (remember as in putting yourself back together properly). Thirdly, it helps you to work out what in your life you don't want to focus on any more.

Sometimes the word 'gratitude' sets up such a reaction in people that it's easier to ask them to find things they 'appreciate.' Choose your preferred word; they are equally as effective.

If you want fast results, write out 100 things that you already have and that you are grateful for every night for a week. They can be the same things or different ones or a mixture of the two. If you have any problem with coming up with 100 Thank Yous, then it simply means that the exercise is even more necessary!

Very simple gratitudes/appreciations are the best, such as being thankful for the ability to see, to hear, to speak, to walk, to touch. Then there is thankfulness for the sky above or autumn leaves or physical health. You can go to the sublime such as chocolate profiteroles or the ridiculous in that you've managed to get rid of the dog's fleas at last. It really can be fun!

To make it easier, you can start with these five senses. Try saying 'Thank You' for:

♦ Ten things you enjoy looking at.

♦ Ten things you enjoy listening to.

♦ Ten things you enjoy touching or feeling.

♦ Ten things you like to eat.

♦ Ten lovely scents.

There you have 50 'Thank Yous' before you even start with a nice cup of tea; sunshine or the gift of laughter. The gratitudes can be for things as small and simple as you like.

Now, it would take a doctorate in Prosperity Training to say 'thanks!' with some sincerity for the fact that someone's just pranged your car or a bird has done what comes naturally on the shoulder of your favourite jacket. It's a tough one sometimes because our parents or grandparents may have schooled us in the belief that we 'ought' to be grateful for things that we never wanted nor asked for and we can be very resistant (quite rightly) to insincere gratitude. Pretty well everyone has, at some time, had to say 'thank you' to an Auntie Freda or an Uncle Phil for a gift that was worse than useless.

The interesting point there is, why are they giving you something so naff? The answer could be that they don't know anything about you or what your tastes are. So, perhaps that problem could be solved with a phone call or a letter where you tell them a bit about who you are and what you like. You never know, they might take the hint and then you could appreciate the fact that you sorted that problem out!

LIKE ATTRACTS LIKE

It's also worth applying the gratitudes idea at work. If you feel bad about your job and just want to get out of a difficult situation but don't put any positive energy into the old job or the search for a new one, then be assured that the next job will contain all the same problems, even if the boss has a different face.

So do what you can to make your work joyful as well as the rest of your life. Just smiling at people can help. Don't bitch about work, don't spread malicious gossip and don't run people down. Remember, what you put out, you get back. Bitch about your job and your job will be a bitch back to you. If you genuinely think that something is wrong, do something about it. Don't just mutter and grumble. To be true to yourself you have to have the courage of your convictions. However, be gentle. It is rarely true to yourself to step on someone else's toes or push their buttons deliberately.

Find every ounce of enjoyment that you can in work (even if it's just chatting with others, putting up pictures you like or having plants or flowers around you) and the Universe will notice that you believe that you deserve something good and give it to you. Try it.

Even difficult relationships (particularly difficult relationships!) can also be something for which we can be grateful, even though it may take us some time to appreciate them fully—but it's a good idea to duck if you say that to anyone's face when they've just been dumped.

I remember my ex-husband saying to a mutual friend that I must surely realise that his decision to leave was best for me as well as for him. He was absolutely right but it was quite natural that it took me a little time to acknowledge that!

I'm certainly grateful for all the prosperity work I learnt with Jonathon when I was with him as it did give me an excellent foundation for developing my own work later. And his leaving showed me very clearly that I wasn't energetically up to speed with my own beliefs!

No matter how hard we may resist the idea, every difficult relationship that we have is an opportunity to learn more about ourselves and others. Quite often, the lesson is not to put up with so much crap! If you think that someone has behaved like an utter bastard to you, then why did you allow them into your life in the first place? Where did you not notice what they were like, where did you stop taking care of yourself or start accepting second best—or where did you let yourself down by not communicating with them or by being unfair to them so that they reacted against you? Hard lessons but, if they are learnt, they can lead to a life of much greater happiness.

The very least that The Bastard can teach you is that you absolutely deserve something better. 'Thanks mate—I'm outta here!' And when you're married to that gorgeous, sexy, kind and loving person with homes in Malibu and the South of France, you'll be appreciative all right! And he (or she) is far more likely to turn up if you start being thankful now.

In a steady relationship, being grateful for your partner's good points can strengthen love. It can even turn a bad relationship around and re-kindle passion.

Occasionally, even an ailing marriage can be saved if the partners look for the good in each other and bless that instead of searching for division and focusing all their attention on what is wrong. Can't think of anything to be grateful for in your partner? Have they been an axe-murderer lately? No? Well, start with that! Start anywhere you can—but start now.

You don't have to do your gratitudes verbally since you don't want to get up people's noses and be too pretentious. Some will be verbal, some mental. If you find you are losing count—great! You have begun to realise what an amazing world we live in and how much we have to be thankful for. Try logging the number of gratitudes for each hour and then add them up at the end of each day. Truly, you will be stunned.

Once you are making gratitude part of your life, you can even try to be grateful for your bills. Our society has been carrying the habit of resentment for being charged for goods we have already used and enjoyed. If your reaction to that is that you do not appreciate using electricity, gas, water or the services of the dustmen, then why not?

Start feeling grateful for the miraculous workings of the world which make it so easy for us to live in warmth and comfort. This will also bring awareness of how much energy we use and may make us make a conscious decision to wear a thicker sweater and turn the heating down. Then you can be grateful for the sweater!

USEFUL AFFIRMATIONS:

I give thanks for a quick and substantial increase in my financial income now.

I bless and appreciate all that I have and look with wonder at its increase now.

Thank you for this wonderful abundant world.

I give thanks for health, happiness, prosperity and joy

Thank you for my healthy eyes, my healthy ears, my healthy nose, my healthy mouth, my healthy throat, my healthy heart… etc (throughout the whole of your body).

EXERCISE:

Say 'thank you' consciously to everyone you can. Look them in the eye and mean it. Watch their response.

EXERCISE:

Think of ten things that you appreciate every time you stop for a cup of tea or coffee or are waiting in a queue.

EXERCISE:

Find something that you think is beautiful and contemplate it for five full minutes, appreciating it in depth. If you give it your full concentration you will feel a shift inside and experience genuine love for the item—and feel the equivalent love and Grace flowing into you.

GIVING

Some people give too much—and others give too little. Women, particularly, tend to over-give to other people so that they end up depleting themselves and then get upset when others don't return the love that they are giving out.

When people over-give to others the Universe thinks (of course) that they would rather give than receive, so it just provides a lot more chances to give and nothing in return.

The trouble with a lot of giving is that it is not unconditional; it is a 'trained response' where we have been taught to take care of others before ourselves. This is also a way of asking for love or even trying to control other people. Although we are taught constantly that it is 'good to give,' any kind of giving that leads to resentment is unhelpful all round—and it is a misinterpretation of spiritual teaching.

Jesus of Nazareth was quoting the Old Testament when he said 'Love your neighbour as you love yourself' and the importance of that phrase is the 'as you love yourself' bit which means that your love for yourself and for others needs to be equal. And that means not over-giving.

To do too little for others over-stretches them and makes them do too much. But to do too much for others disempowers them so that they do not know how to take care of themselves properly.

So do try only to give when you *want* to give and not out of guilt or the wish to impress others. Gifts from guilt or ego will invalidate the love that needs to go with giving and make the gift conditional. If you habitually give to beggars, practice walking past one without giving. Just being aware of the layers of guilt is a good test of whether you are giving out of genuine love or because you are afraid not to. Who are you afraid of? The beggar, God or yourself?

It is also worth thinking of this: in holistic medicine, cancer is commonly thought of as a disease of 'nice' people; people who don't use the word 'no.' Breast cancer is a case in point but most cancers would also appear to follow this rule. In astrology, the planet Jupiter is about expansion and giving out—and it also rules tumours. Tumours are where tissues in the body over-expand and become harmful to us. Maybe the over-nurturing of others is a psychological factor in cancer sufferers?

I know of one lady with breast cancer who got up at 2am to drive more than 50 miles to rescue her adult son whose car had broken down on the motorway. What kind of monster had she nurtured in that young man? Not only was he not prepared to get himself some kind of road cover for his car, he was willing to have his mother go to such lengths when she was seriously ill. She hadn't helped him to be an individual through all her love and caring. The lady died, putting everyone else first to the last minute and apologising for being any trouble...

Also, much heart disease (which has been growing more common in women since we began balancing career and home) often stems from an over-expanded, congested heart. Of course, there is also the opposite— the contracted heart which may find it difficult to love; we harden our hearts against people or events and our arteries follow suit. I think it is worth watching our levels of giving and receiving carefully if we have a family history of cancer or heart disease.

There are three levels of Giving in the Bible (they are known as Tithing). They go in this order:

1. — Give to God/spiritual growth.

2. — Give to yourself for celebration.

3. — Give to others.

Most people get the order wrong; they give to others first. People with prosperity issues often say 'I give! I give my time.' That's fine—but all you will get back from that is other people giving you their time. Very nice, too, but not the point if you're strapped for cash.

How do you give to God? The old way was to give to the Temple in the Temple Tithe because that paid the priests whose job was to remind you of the wonders of the Oral Teaching. You gave as a thanks-offering to God for helping to live your life happily.

Spiritual insurance, in fact. It does work; if we give to the good experiences in life then far fewer of the bad experiences will come our way.

'Why should I pay insurance to God?' you may say. 'That's not fair! Why shouldn't it all be unconditional?' It is and you don't have to. It doesn't affect God in the slightest whether you give to It or not; God doesn't have a bank account as such, nor the need for one. Giving to God affects you; it acknowledges the Source of all Things and, if you acknowledge that the Source is also the source of money and give abundance your attention, the Law will make it true for you and give you money and abundance back.

Another way to give to the Divine is to give towards your spiritual growth, so it's just as valid to put your first tithe towards something which brings you closer to God, such as a book or a workshop.

TITHING TO GOD

The idea is that we give 10 per cent of our 'increase' which means whatever we earn.

This appears a little steep to us in the 21st century when our 'increase' is taken up with mortgages, fuel bills, travel, food costs etc. And it's fair to say that in ancient days most people were self-sufficient, or nearly so, and their tithes were just as frequently made in sheep, harvested food or woven goods. A tenth most probably meant 'one whole thing' in a world where they didn't do much counting. One whole thing could mean an egg, a basket of fruit or a sheep.

The principle behind tithing is a good one and I have experience that it works. However, the most important lesson in tithing is; *don't even think about doing it unless you truly want to*. Tithing because you think you *ought* to doesn't work and can damage your relationship with both God and money or, if it does work, the results will come back slowly and reluctantly, in just the same way as the money went out.

So don't tithe if you know you could end up using it as another tool for beating yourself up.

It's fine to give time too if you want time back but giving time is unlikely to bring back anything other than time.

The questions which come up immediately are 'Why?' and 'How?'

TITHING — WHY?

'Why' is because by putting God first you actually take care of yourself; at least, that's the theory. The idea dates back to the story of Jacob wrestling with the angel in Genesis. Jacob vowed to give the first ten per cent of his increase to God in a kind of contract with the Holy One. In return, God protected and prospered Jacob. Charles and Myrtle Fillmore, the founders of

Unity Church, wrote out a covenant with God and they and their church prospered as a direct result.

The money given to God or towards spiritual growth seems to ensure that tithers are protected from difficult situations so that their lives seem to flow more easily. And more money comes back to them. The idea is that God pays back to you ten times what you give to God, which sounds like a pretty good investment deal to me. It is not a system that is meant to take money away from you but one which gives back to you in money, health, strength and grace.

Tithing is a big step to take, all the same. Many spiritual teachers recommend that those who want to try tithing do so a little at a time, e.g. one per cent, building up to ten per cent if/when that feels comfortable. I say give what you can when you can but never worry about the percentage.

The Catherine Ponder books in the bibliography are excellent on the subject of tithing but they do tend to bang on a bit about it and there appears to be an almost subliminal suggestion that you tithe to Dr. Ponder's own church. She is always very appreciative if you do and she sends you regular newsletters about prosperity, which are very helpful, but it's important to remember that you don't have to tithe to people because they are the ones who told you about tithing!

TITHING — HOW?

Which brings us on to the 'How?' part of tithing.

The answer is to give to the person or institution which inspires you and which makes you feel closest to God. This is *not* the same as giving to charity and it is *not* about giving to your own church/temple/synagogue as a regular donation or as a fee for membership. Tithing is a very personal and special thing.

Don't be put off if the person to whom you wish to

tithe is rich. In fact, if you are doing prosperity work, it would be most surprising if you did want to tithe to someone who was not prosperous themselves! If they're not abundant, how can they inspire you? Giving to those who need money is different; that's the third tithe.

You can tithe anonymously if you wish. That is said to be the highest form of giving because it means that there can be no direct gratitude in return for the gift and therefore it has to be unconditional.

You will soon find out if you tithed to the 'wrong' person. I once tithed anonymously to a teacher of mine who then told a meeting that I attended that someone had sent her some money and how angry she was about it. She said that she did not charge for spiritual work and that she felt insulted.

Later on in the same talk the teacher said how much she and her husband needed finance to move to a bigger home and that they were continually asking God for the money. I quietly left the meeting, having realised that I was no longer inspired by that particular teacher. An expensive mistake perhaps—but as the money was given unconditionally, not feeling bad about it was an important lesson too. That one took a little time to digest!

Quite often, when people are not certain whether they have tithed to 'the right' sources of inspiration— or they were simply feeling very short of money—the cheque got lost in the post or was just never cashed. Sometimes God gives back pretty fast!

It's also okay to tithe to yourself or to a friend if you feel either of you have been pretty darn brilliant this month and, of course, to put the money towards any event or product that will genuinely increase your spiritual knowledge and delight.

No one can prove the benefits of tithing because the whole idea is that it is a kind of insurance policy. So, when nothing bad happens, you don't realise what you may have missed!

However, regular tithers have reported back instances such as not getting flu when the whole of the rest of the office was ill and being passed over for redundancy when it was their turn. Others who wanted redundancy got it!

A friend of mine who tithes got a kind of 'cosmic nudge' to take his car in for a service a month earlier than he had planned. The garage discovered that the bolts which held the engine in the car were just about to shear off which would have badly damaged the engine. Even a few more days would have been serious, if not dangerous, not to mention hideously expensive.

In another case, when a woman tithed £10 her husband gave her a pair of pearl and diamond earrings worth more than £100 for her birthday the following week. She later discovered that her husband had been intending to buy her something much cheaper but had seen the earrings at almost the exact time that she sent off her tithe — and he couldn't resist buying them.

GIVING TO YOURSELF

This is **Deuteronomy 14:26** on the second tithe:

'And thou shalt bestow that money for whatsoever thy soul lusteth after, for oxen, or for sheep, or for wine, or for strong drink, or for whatsoever thy soul desireth: and thou shalt eat there before the LORD thy God, and thou shalt rejoice, thou, and thine household.'

Strong drink eh? Apart from anything else, wine is an essential part of the beautiful Jewish Sabbath Eve ceremony on a Friday night.

The 'celebration tithe' was traditionally a way of putting money aside to attend festivals and holy feast days. In our society that means Summer holidays as well as festivals such as Diwali, Hannukah or Christmas. Certainly, putting money aside for these is a great way to take care of yourself but it is also a good idea to buy yourself little presents on a regular basis. All too often we take care of others' needs and then wonder why no one buys us flowers or a special gift.

It is worth checking how often you pay the bills *before* you even buy yourself a bunch of flowers or a decent bottle of wine. Well, stop it! The miracle of tithing is that if you *do* put God and fun first, there is always enough to pay those bills. After all, your children still get their everyday needs taken care of and they certainly spend their money on the things they want!

If you pay the bills first and neglect yourself, that good old Karmic Law kicks in again and the Universe just thinks you want bills and debts to be more important than you are—and keeps on giving you more of them. It's about balance; don't neglect your obligations but value yourself too.

Even if you are feeling broke you can still treat yourself to a bar of chocolate or a magazine that you enjoy. And the secret with that is to take the time to enjoy them properly instead of rushing them or fitting them into space that belongs to someone else. Then the Universe knows that you are willing to take time out for pleasure.

If you put a certain amount of money aside each month for your own personal development or for a complementary medicine session, it is a wonderful statement of self-worth and it will certainly make life happier and more prosperous.

GIVING TO OTHERS

This is the most easily understood of the three levels of giving but, even so, it needs a little explanation. This is giving to those in need—rather than giving because we want to be loved.

It also involves giving what is needed, when it is needed rather than what we want to give. We may be happy to give time and attention but what may be needed is practical help or money.

When I was widowed in my 30s a friend asked what he could do, practically, to help and I said, 'could you mow the lawn?' For some reason, mowing the lawn was one of the things which was quite beyond me at the time and the grass was already about six inches high.

The friend rang me up five weeks later and offered to come round and mow the lawn. I had done it myself twice in that time so I didn't need his help by then and that ended up with him feeling that his help was unwanted and me feeling resentful that it had taken him so long to get round to it.

Nowadays, hopefully, I'm more specific in my requests if I need help. But it is worth checking out what others truly need and when they need it before you offer to give.

Play with these three levels; don't do anything that makes you feel too uncomfortable. But do remember that a little discomfort is to be expected when we do something new—all change feels odd. Spiritual growth is rarely entirely comfortable. But whatever and however you give, try not to give yourself a hard time over it!

CLEAR OUT YOUR CLUTTER!

Clutter-clearing is all the rage nowadays and most of us do realise that holding on to old pictures, books, letters, grudges, clothes etc. does have an effect on life at all levels.

So many times when people say they want to be more prosperous, the weight of the energy on old 'stuff' in their homes prevents them from doing so. If you remember that prosperity and money are energies that flow like a river, any kind of dam will create problems in the long run.

Clearing out clutter is the bit about the 'rich man and the eye of the needle' from the New Testament. It *is* hard to enter into the Kingdom of God when you are possessed.

It's an interesting word, 'possession.' The balance is about having beautiful things in your life which you can let go of any time you need to do so—rather than having your possessions possess you.

The rich man in the parable said he wanted to follow Jesus but he wasn't ready to give anything up in order to do so. Plenty of people get fired up when they hear an inspirational speaker; not as many are willing to pay up for the workshop afterwards—even if they do, it can be hard to tell their friends and family that they are on a new path which will give them the knowledge to change their lives for real.

Jesus himself was an itinerant preacher, wise enough in the Laws of Prosperity to know that everywhere he went he would be taken care of, fed and offered a bed for the night. He could manifest whatever he wanted wherever he was (including the money to pay his taxes); he was a Master and those who followed him were in training to be the same. They couldn't just stay in one place and they couldn't carry their possessions with them. But they also didn't have complicated lives like ours so they didn't get the opportunity to collect clutter the way we can.

I had a seminal experience as a part of my great Montana emigration experience where there came a point where I was standing at Seattle airport with two suitcases, a laptop computer and a Beagle. I had no home; no job; no car; no keys. I didn't even know if I still had a marriage. I was totally free and I could have gone anywhere in the world. Amazingly, I did realise what an extraordinary moment it was and what incredible choices I was being offered.

My greatest teacher, comforter and support at that time was the small, furry creature by my side. She was always full of the calm acceptance that wherever I went was her home too; she had no possessions but it never worried her in the slightest; she knew that she would be taken care of, fed and loved until the day she went back to the great soul of Beagle. She was right.

If you live in an environment which is filled with clutter, it is almost impossible for any new good stuff to find its way in to your life. And it is not just the physical possessions that tie people down; the mental and emotional connections do too.

But can you actually identify your clutter? Do you realise that it is as simple as a desk continually covered in papers and empty coffee mugs or a room full of furniture and ornaments?

There is also the diary full of appointments which leaves no time for you to do what you truly want to do; or an address book filled with names of people you really don't like enough to contact. Would you put these under the heading of clutter? Please do!

Clutter can be defined as *anything* that gets in the

way of your doing what you what you want to do—
anything that blocks energy flow in you, in your life or
in your physical space. It can sometimes be the things
that you feel you have to do because that gets in the
way of doing something that brings you joy.

WHAT TO DO—OR NOT

There's an old adage: have nothing in your home that
is neither beautiful nor useful. So anything that you
consider to be either is not clutter. But please be really
honest with yourself. The things that *might* come in
handy are dangerously borderline!

It may be easy to tidy out a drawer, for example, but
to go through a house or an office takes time, energy
and commitment.

Be kind to yourself while you clear stuff out; some
people do it in one fell swoop and others need to do it
slowly and gently. Plan to take a carrier bag-full to a
charity shop each time you go shopping or to spend an
hour a week throwing stuff out. It doesn't have to be
any more than that to get on a roll.

Get a good friend to help with the job, too; they'll
be more dispassionate than you about what needs to go
and what doesn't.

Nature abhors a vacuum—and the laws of physics
state that energy cannot be destroyed, only transformed.
So it is wise to ensure that when you do clear clutter,
you don't immediately replace it with something just
as daft or useless!

Here's a good clutter-clearing system as defined by my
friend Barbara Palmer:

First, get one or two black bags, some carrier bags
and a box. Define the area that you are going to clear—
and stick to that. Sort the contents of the area/drawer/
cupboard into the following:

♦ Beautiful and/or useful objects you want to keep.

♦ Objects that you don't want, even though there is nothing wrong with them and they may come in useful someday.

♦ Things that are broken but could be mended.

♦ Things that are broken beyond economic repair (I know, I know! Why would anyone not have thrown these away already? Probably because some part of their psyche genuinely believes that it might be possible to use them or some part from them sometime in the future when the world economy has failed completely!).

♦ Things that should be somewhere else in the house/office.

♦ Don't knows.

Things that you don't want could be sold to raise some immediate prosperity; given to a charity shop; even given as presents (just because you don't want them doesn't mean that they aren't desirable). If they were gifts to you, then you could take a photo and keep that instead!

If something is broken and just been put away, it is unlikely that you will use it even if it is mended, as you may already have replaced it—or you don't need it anyway. Do you want to repair it? Could it be sold or given away if it is mended and would it be worth spending time and money on it? Is there some organisation that would arrange repairs and then sell or give it to someone else who could use it? Or would all that represent a load of clutter in your timetable?

Many of us have been brought up in difficult circumstances or by parents who lived through the Second World War when 'make do and mend' was absolutely essential. Nowadays, built-in obsolescence is the norm, most things are easily available and you may not have the skills or the time to mend anything anyway. It may also be time to cultivate the belief that you can have what you want when you want it which allows you to release things when they cease to be of use.

However, when you do come across the tights/hold-ups/socks that are sitting in a drawer waiting for you to sew up the hole in the foot, it truly now is time either to do just that—or to throw them away!

The black bags are for things that should be thrown away, carrier bags or boxes for things that can go to charity. Don't forget that some charities can use clothes for many things, not just re-sale. What isn't saleable in the UK can be sent abroad as aid and what cannot be used for clothing anymore can be sold to the rag industry—cotton for paper-making and others for industrial wipes. So, even if that tee-shirt is totally disreputable it could turn up in some jazzy re-cycled paper somewhere.

Most prosperity teachers recommend that you get rid of any clothes that you haven't worn in 12 months—but I don't think this is necessarily reasonable in the UK where the weather is so unpredictable. It would be a shame to throw out a good winter coat simply because there hasn't been any snow for years. Anyway, there is a proviso that if something is lovely or gives you joy it should be retained anyway.

However, do watch out for the 'I'll wear it when I've lost that weight' trap. I've fallen for that one many a time, having been convinced that those four or five pounds would magically disappear. Sometimes they do... but if it gets to be a major weight-loss that's required, grit your teeth and get rid of the clothes. After all, if you do become svelte again, you'll be so thrilled you'll almost certainly want to go out and get new and fashionable stuff anyway.

Don't be surprised if you start feeling emotional when all these hidden things come to the surface. If there's stuff which came into your life or which you used at a time of emotional pain or anger, it will be charged with some of the energy of that time. This is one of the reasons why it is better to 'salami slice' this job; the physical effort may be tiring enough but the emotions may come up and hit you for six. Better to experience the emotion and let it go than suppress it again by covering it up in work or avoiding it.

You may even need to have a good cry. Go to it—and give yourself a treat afterwards. However, if any stuff makes you cry, please consider seriously whether to get rid of it because doing so may well help to resolve the situation—*unless* it is special stuff from someone you loved who died recently. I know from experience that that can be very different. It is quite tempting to get rid of your late partner or friend's possessions too soon so, if you are adamant that you want them out of your home quickly because of the pain they represent, I would suggest that you ask your Mum or someone close to keep them for you in a box for at least a year. Then you can go back and make a more dispassionate decision later on when the world has rebalanced itself a little.

Whenever it is difficult to choose what to do about some potential clutter, it can be put in a box and left for a time. Decide whether to review it in a month or two or six and make a note in your diary for that time. If you have not wanted anything from the box during that period, it should be disposed of.

However, do realise that your subconscious can be very powerful here and may make decisions for you. When my ex-husband left me, I asked my best friend to put some special things, including our framed wedding picture, somewhere safe for me while I got over the first shock and grief. She did so—and a week or so later, when I was round at her place, I managed to trip over and kick the box where the special things were kept, smashing the picture completely.

It is not unknown for some instant prosperity to turn up when clearing clutter; a banknote appears in the pocket of a jacket or a passbook for an account you'd forgotten, as well as finding things you've mislaid.

CLUTTERING PEOPLE

To clear out the clutter in your address book, you need to sit quietly and review each person whose details are in there. If your heart lifts or remains neutral when you think of them, you can leave the address in the book. If you feel your heart sink, then cross the address out— but cross it out in pencil because the feeling may not be permanent and you can review it again next year. If it is someone who you really know that you never want to see or hear from again, cross his or her name out in pen.

Sometimes we feel awful about letting a former friend go—it seems really mean, especially if that person is unhappy or doesn't have many other friends. But it's worth considering that, with you in their life, they are actually being short-changed in having a 'friend' around who doesn't really like them. If you weren't there, they would have the opportunity to find space for someone who might love them very much more.

It might also wake them up a little to realise that you have changed and moved on. Maybe it is time that they did too? If you do decide to ease a former friend out of your life, please don't do it by adding hurt to their lives or blaming them—and certainly not with a 'Dear John' letter. Just ease yourself away as gently as you can. If they are angry with you and want to pull you back then the two of you do need to talk but, very often, they are going to be just as happy to see you go as you are to leave.

If you believe that your relationship with your partner, husband or wife has become clutter, however, you really do owe it to them—and to yourself—to talk it over with them. If you can explain how you feel and if you are willing to see if the relationship can be healed rather than just throwing it away, you may be able to recapture the spark that brought you together. Any marriage is worth trying to save if you get the opportunity because the debris and pain of broken relationships is clutter of a colossal kind. However, the partnership must be rebuilt, not just continued with the cracks papered over...

For a cluttered diary, you could cross through pages in the weeks ahead with yellow highlighter or write 'no' in yellow highlighter across the page. This is easy to write over in pen but helps you stop and consider whether you want to make the suggested appointment. The best time-management systems start with your allocating time to the important things in your life and only then set time for business appointments and tasks. When asked, most executives will say that the most important thing in their life is their family but you often can't tell that by the way they lead their lives.

It is very often at the funerals of friends and family that people realise that they haven't lived their lives the way they wanted to—and it is perfectly true that no one on their deathbed says 'I wish I'd spent more time at the office.'

Look at the things that you feel that you *have* to do and see if you can make the distinction between important, urgent and busy-work. Oddly enough, 'urgent' is usually less important than important—it just feels as if it should be done first. And 'busy-work' is all those things that you 'simply must do' in order to get out of doing the other two!

Is it possible to delegate tasks to someone else or not do them at all? Asking others to do something will help them to grow and it really doesn't matter if things are not done perfectly for a time. Honest it doesn't! A former boss of mine taught me a lot when he said: 'If you ask for the wall to be painted green, there's no use in griping if it's not painted a shade that you like. As long as it's green, the job has been done and done well.'

Some of the things that you think you *have* to do don't add anything to the sum of human happiness; going to religious services when you would rather be walking in fields is not helping either God or you... and 'supporting' friends when you really don't want to be there is adding negative, not positive, energies to their endeavours.

Habits can also be clutter. If you really enjoy doing bungee jumping, horse riding, sewing class or whatever, even if everyone else thinks you're daft, then just carry on doing it. But if you are doing it because someone else thinks you should or because you haven't got anything better to do, then a re-think is needed!

If you are doing something because your mother did it, remember that she may be doing it because *her* mother did it and for no other reason. Ask her if you can. Horribly often, people discover that the parent who influenced them so strongly that—for example—shoes must be cleaned *that* way, discover years later that their Mum or Dad found a new way after the children left home and changed their own habits perfectly cheerfully.

Remember, times change and what was appropriate then may not be appropriate now, given your lifestyle, new materials etc. Also, remember that lots of people value *you*, not what you do or how you do it.

FAT AS CLUTTER

Excess weight can be a form of clutter, literally because it can make it difficult to move easily and freely through the world and, also, because it is often used as an excuse to put life on hold—for instance, not joining a club or class until weight is lost. It can also be an excuse for not being in a relationship or a barrier to intimacy within an existing relationship.

Tough words—and I would be the first to admit that I'm not always as slim as I would like to be so I'll own up that I haven't got this one entirely solved myself. Usually the secret is to accept who you are, even if you wouldn't be asked to pose as a model. Better to be a chubby happy person in clothes a size larger than you'd like than a chubby, unhappy, person holding her tummy in all day.

Most women, unless they are one of the naturally skinny types, fluctuate within about half a stone throughout any given year. That's fine and normal, even if it is irritating at times! It is in our nature to want to be what we are not—look at those with curly hair envying those with straight and *vice versa*. There probably isn't a self-help book in existence that doesn't tell us that the secret, the whole secret and nothing but the secret, is to love and accept ourselves exactly as we are.

However, if you are seriously overweight then there

may well be a psychological issue which is cluttering up your life as much as the extra fat. The odds are that you don't eat that much—extreme fatties rarely do. But your body has got some mixed messages going on and these probably come from some pain in the past or some erroneous belief in your cells. If you can get some help from a homoeopath or a counsellor it will probably be easier and more effective than see-saw dieting—which only makes you feel awful anyway! ‿

FORGIVING

Holding onto the pain of past relationships or people who 'done you wrong' is also clutter. It takes a huge amount of energy not to forgive someone no matter how tempting it might be! It means that you hold onto the pain and the anger and that uses up much-needed space for love in your heart and your mind. Truly!

I'm not suggesting for one moment that you forgive wrongs too early (it is very important to honour and express feelings of hurt and anger) but do try to remember that to forgive simply means to give up the pain. It does not mean that you condone the behaviour that hurt you. Not at all!

My friend Ed has a great saying: 'Never assume malice where you can impute stupidity.' So much of what others do to us which hurts us is all about them and very little about us. It's hard to remember that when you've been badly wounded, but Eleanor Roosevelt made a good point when she said that no one could make us feel inadequate without our permission. A lot of unforgiveness is about hurt pride more than anything else.

When we are hurt it is important to shout, scream and cry and get the emotion out but it is also important to create spaces for happiness where we can begin to let go of that hurt. Nursing it and using it as a weapon may be tempting but it destroys us, not the one we want to hurt. Apart from anything else, two wrongs don't make a right.

But take it at your own pace. I remember, at one workshop, a woman became quite anxious about this and asked how long it would be 'permissible' not to forgive someone who had left her. I asked her how long ago the break-up had taken place and she replied 'two weeks ago.'

It can take two years! It can take more than that! But, if you are not beginning to move on *at all* after one year has passed, then do get help because you are beginning to hurt yourself. Sometimes it will take a whole lifetime to clear out all the pain but, as long as you can see distinct progress towards letting the problem go as each month passes, you are on the right track.

And don't add beating yourself up to the pain you are already dealing with!

Remember, again, that prosperity flows like a river and, if it is dammed or blocked, it cannot work properly. Also that nature abhors a vacuum. Clear out that clutter, lose the excess or the pain and watch the new and good come in.

USEFUL AFFIRMATIONS:

I let go and let God.

I am willing to forgive, I am willing to release everything that blocks my good.

I am willing to live a simpler, happier and more prosperous life.

I loose and let go. I let go and trust.

EXERCISE:

Designate just one drawer to be cleared on a certain day

EXERCISE:

Organise a 'clutter swap-shop' with some friends. You all bring a bag of things you no longer want to one person's house, lay them out and choose new and different things instead of your old unwanted ones. One of you does need to commit to taking the stuff wanted by none of you to a charity shop the next day.

EXERCISE:

Check your energy levels with your friends. Do you end a conversation or come away from a visit happy and energised—or do you feel drained? Some people are 'psychic vampires' drawing energy from others. If you have people in your life like that (including family) limit your time with them. Also take flower essences such as *Bach Flower Remedy* **Walnut** or *Australian Flower Remedy* **Fringed Violet** for psychic protection.

IMAGE, EGO AND SOCIAL SITUATIONS

The human Ego is a funny thing. Basically, it is formed by habits and patterns. The Jesuits had a saying: 'Give me a child until he is seven and he is mine for life' because the human Ego develops over the first seven years of our lives and we tend to keep the beliefs that we formed up until then. So many of the beliefs we have and the patterns we run date back to our earliest years.

Some of these, such as 'look both ways before you cross the road,' are still very useful but a lot of our subconscious beliefs are very inhibiting when it comes to prosperity work.

Mystics teach that the Ego is meant to be the servant of the Self. This means that our real selves should dictate consciously what the Ego will run through habit. This works well when you learn to drive a car—the Self learns how to do the driving fully consciously and then hands it over to the Ego to do on automatic. It is the Ego that remembers to breathe and how to walk; that dresses us in the morning, gets our breakfast, does all the routine jobs and daily maintenance; it is the Self that is kick-started into action when there is a crisis or anything new happens. The Ego does not like 'new' because it has no recognition of it. That's why there can be so much resistance to change both within and around us.

Prosperity work is about coming from the Self, deciding what is true for us now and re-training the Ego to be as prosperous as we wish ourselves to be instead of telling us that it's 'not right' or that we 'don't deserve it.'

Money does not come to people because they deserve it. The idea of 'deserving' is a complete irrelevance to any form of energy; it just comes where it is attracted. So you don't have to deserve the money you have; you just have to have a mind that is open to receiving prosperity. That applies whether you are a bank robber or an holistic therapist. You may have other Karmic issues to deal with but, unless that Karma is directly to do with serious misuse of money, it won't affect your ability to be wealthy.

However, your attitude to others who already are prosperous *does* affect what abundance comes to you. Do you envy very rich people now? Do you think that they should be so wealthy for what they do? Do you think that they got their money fairly? Do you think that they use it well? Or do 'fat cats' drive you crazy?

Do you snarl when you see someone in a BMW or a 4x4 (especially if they are driving badly) or feel jealous when you see someone who, in your view, has very little talent paraded all over a magazine, showing off their personally trained and expensively dieted body and their obvious financial wealth?

If you have issues with any of these thoughts, there is likely to be a sneaky inner belief that, if you were that rich, others would feel the same about you. That's a real blocker on prosperity no matter how talented you might be.

More than that, the Universe just reads your emotions at the time. It knows that we are all connected at the level of the collective unconscious and any negative thought about another is also a negative thought about us. The Universe doesn't discriminate; it just sees disapproval of money, so it doesn't hand any over. Simple as that.

I knew a very talented graphic artist who always sniped at the work of others. Ask him to comment on a website, an exhibition or a book design and he would almost certainly tell you that it is rubbish. If you asked him to do work for you he wouldn't let his 'artistic credibility' be challenged so wouldn't do what you ask him to do—and he charged exorbitant rates for his talents that chased away most of his potential clients. In the end, he stopped doing his art because 'nobody appreciated it.'

However, since I first wrote this book, he has discovered prosperity consciousness through the Abraham-Hicks teachings. It has truly transformed him through helping him to see that the Law of Attraction meant that the world *had* to be reflected back to him in his own mirror. It was his own self-hatred that he was projecting onto the world and, in learning that, he was able to start looking for the good both in and around him. Not only is he much happier, with a lot more friends, but he is working again and his work is selling …

For the rest of us who don't have a specific talent, there is still a fear that, if we shine, we will be knocked down by our friends or the media in the same way as other people who are 'no better than they should be' are attacked in gossip and magazines. We fear being judged as we have either judged others or observed them being judged. You only have to see the media's attitude towards a new 'star' to see our pattern. The 'star' is created by the people and loved by the people and then we start to chop away at them; we buy magazines which show them looking unkempt, too skinny, too fat or with too much cellulite, with banner headlines sniping at their imperfections.

Closer to home, do you have any friends to whom it is hard to talk when you've had a stroke of good fortune? Do you play down what you are doing because they won't approve, even if it's only in a hidden, subtle way?

Then there's the guilt about of being wealthy when there are so many poor and starving people in the world. Excuse the bluntness but that one really is a cop out! How can you help the poor and starving if you are poor and starving yourself? It is those people who are sufficiently wealthy to give who can give the most help to those in need.

And, if all that wasn't enough, there's the issue of your parents; whether you are conforming or rebelling and whether they will judge you as becoming 'better than you should be' if you do succeed.

So, what's to do in the midst of all this opposition?

There's only one answer that I know of and that's 'do it anyway.' Don't take any excrement from anyone about building your own path in your own way in your own direction. It is better to make your own way (and your own mistakes) than to live life in the pockets of other people's opinions. It's your life and nobody else should be living it for you.

I know that it's easier said than done but you can start in very subtle ways and build up your confidence in yourself slowly. The more you do this, the more you will tell the Universe that you honour and respect financial wealth.

♦ Each time you see the starlet or the person with the flash car, practice smiling and saying 'Good for them. I'll have some of that too, please!'

♦ If a friend has something you envy, tell them honestly (in a voice with laughter in it if you can!) that you are so jealous you could spit—but that you are totally delighted for them. Much better than seething in silence and creating a block between you.

♦ When others knock the rich and famous don't join in. Instead say 'Not my truth. I bless them and their wealth' under your breath.

♦ Look for pictures of lovely houses in estate agents' windows and look for the car you would really like in a posh car showroom, and say 'that's for me too.'

♦ Tidy up what you already have—clean and polish your car, for example.

♦ Window shop in the best stores.

♦ Work out a list of exquisite small gifts that you can ask for at Christmas or for birthdays—and give other people quality gifts too. That will get other people used to the idea that you expect quality.

♦ Read *Vogue* or *Country Life* and other 'posh' magazines at the library if you don't want to buy them yourself.

♦ Cut out soap operas and any TV shows where people are belittled or shown accepting any kind of bad behaviour (though stick with your favourite comedies—whatever makes you laugh is good).

It may surprise you to realise that Cosmic Law works for personal appearance just as much as what is in your heart. It notes what you wear and where you pass your time.

Wear clothes that are smart (whatever the fashion). Another 'Grandma-ism' is that one good quality suit and two good shirts is worth a dozen cheap fashionable outfits. If you are into the New Age, then consider carefully the image that you put out. Be aware that to others you may just look impoverished or weird rather than wise and spiritual if you wear floaty bright dresses or cheesecloth shirts. The everyday world's Ego-consciousness exists and it does make snap judgments, whether we like it or not. The great task for people in Spiritual work is to be 'in the world but not of it' and that means fitting in where it's necessary — like if you want to get that job. You are not compromising yourself; you are accepting what is and agreeing to work with it; you can attempt to change things, if you want to, once you are inside.

It is not about trying to make yourself something that you are not — or about showing off or being vain — but about showing your true value to the world.

It is certainly very important to be true to yourself but we all have to take other people into consideration, too. You may be able to get out of your Ego into your Self but there is no guarantee that anybody else can or even wants to. So there is no point in turning up for an interview for a 'visible' job in a bank or somewhere similar in torn jeans and with a ring through your nose. You may like the look but you won't get hired. An Internet Company might think differently — but do check first.

It's also good to give out the impression that you are prosperous even if you think that you aren't. Far better to have one good quality smart outfit than several cheap ones which look tatty after a few outings.

Whether we like it or not, the world runs a mile when it scents weakness or failure. If you want to get a good job or start a business you need to exude confidence and quality. Clean clothes, hair, shoes—all the traditional aspects which our parents and grandparents told us—are the best tools for presenting ourselves in the marketplace for prosperity.

Throw out (or mend) all the socks with holes, the saggy tee-shirts and the shoes that have scuff marks all down the sides. Even in your own private life, check out what you look like to the Universe every day. Take a good look at yourself in the mirror. Do you present a prosperous image? If not, why should the Universe or the people in it take your quest for abundance seriously? Slopping around in a sweatshirt when you're pottering about at home is fine but even so, beware of holes in your clothing, stains or anything which would make you ashamed to open the door to a lover or a movie star.

Work out what it is that you actually want to portray to other people. And then ask other people whether you are portraying it. Alternatively, ask people what your image is—you'll be surprised at their opinion as it may differ violently from yours.

Once you know, then you can act. Do you like what they saw in you? If so, act it! If not, then change your appearance and/or behaviour accordingly.

Most of us have friends who see different sides to us. With some we are more extrovert and with others more thoughtful. Both are aspects of ourselves but they are expressed selectively, to the appropriate people. You wouldn't want to flirt with your sister, just as you wouldn't want to act bored with that attractive person at work.

The choice is up to you; but you will get better prosperity results from eating just one course in a four-star restaurant than you will in going to McDonalds a dozen times. If you want abundance you have to align yourself with it so that the Universe agrees that it is where you belong.

There's a great quotation from Ernest Bramah's book, *The Wallet of Kai Lung*, which sums this up:

'It is a mark of insincerity of purpose to spend one's time in looking for the sacred Emperor in the low-class tea-rooms.'

If you are not feeling prosperous (and even if you are) it's a great idea to go to places where seriously rich people are. In a way, their wealth rubs off on you (by touching auras) and it certainly lifts your sense of your own image. Go to the best hotels in town and linger for an hour over a cup of coffee. That way you get to read all the newspapers for free, you look as if you belong in a smart environment and you have a great time.

The Universe will notice that you think those are the places that you ought to be.

When I got back to the UK from living in America, I found a job as a PA in the centre of London. I found it really hard as I had no experience and everything was very scary. I was also feeling very broke but I used to haunt Fortnum and Mason in my lunch hour as it made me feel better to look at the beautiful foods and clothes and the artefacts. For my Mum's birthday, I bought her a selection of foods from the food hall. It actually cost less than the usual amount that I spent on her presents but everything had 'prosperity' written all over it.

Within six weeks two friends, who knew nothing about this, sent me a Fortnum's hamper as a gift. The Universe had watched and listened and given me exactly what I was giving out.

Nowadays, my office in London is the tea room at a five-star hotel. Two pots of tea with four quality biscuits costs less than £10 and means that my client and I can spend an hour and a half in beautiful surroundings, with live piano music and access to some of the best rest-rooms in England. A *full* afternoon tea is £25, including smoked salmon sandwiches, savouries, cream tea and cakes—and you can eat until you are virtually incapable of movement while being served with elegance and style. Even £25 is a pretty cheap rent for an office in central London!

So go where your purpose is. If you feel broke and you want to mark a special occasion that, choose brunch at a good hotel rather than dinner at a place that doesn't inspire you.

If you don't get gifts or the lifestyle that you want, just check what you are putting out image-wise. It will pay dividends in the long run.

USEFUL AFFIRMATIONS:

I am willing to experience all the wealth and joy the Universe has for me now.

Angels of Prosperity, walk with me, work in me wherever I am, whatever I see.

May I meet the people I need to meet.
May I not meet the people I don't need to meet.
May the people who need to meet me, meet me.
May the people who don't need to meet me not meet me.

I am worthy of the best that the Universe can offer.

EXERCISE:

Clean all your shoes! They are the one thing most frequently forgotten when we spruce ourselves up.

EXERCISE:

Check out the state of the inside of your car and your desk at the office, if you have one. They represent your own self-image and they are sending out messages on your behalf!

EXERCISE:

Ask your friends what image you put out—and be willing to hear what they say!

PERSONAL NOTES & AFFIRMATIONS

MONITORING

If we want more money in our lives, we need to be in touch with what is happening to the money that we already have. Again it's the Universe's habit of taking us literally… if we don't take care of the money that we do have, it will assume that we don't care about it *per se* and don't want any more.

A lot of money problems stem from lack of knowledge of where all the stuff goes every month. We think that we know our outgoing expenses but the truth is that very few people (apart from accountants) really do.

It is important to know where you really stand with regard to money, otherwise everything that you do to bring in more will misfire. You will just spend the extra cash that you've manifested without realising that you are re-creating exactly the same problem.

KNOW YOUR MONEY!

Firstly, get to know the cash itself. Take a long, hard look at the banknotes in your wallet. Learn about them; appreciate them. Do you know what they actually look like? For example:

♦ The UK £20 note has a picture of Adam Smith, author of *The Theory of Moral Sentiments* and *The Wealth of Nations*. A very wise man and a Deist.

♦ The UK £10 note has a humming bird representing the sweetness of life and an image of your ship coming in.

♦ The UK £5 not has an image of Elizabeth Fry on it. She was a Quaker who focused on education for women.

♦ The €10 note has a bridge to encourage you to look ahead on your journey.

♦ Every $US note has the words 'IN GOD WE TRUST' on it.

They are all very positive icons. So, every time you handle a note or a coin, treat it carefully and consider its significance. Wonder about where it came from, how many people it has blessed on its route and how many people may have blessed or cursed it in return. Bless it and you cleanse it from any negative energy. Bless it again as you release it to pay for something that you want so that it takes good energy with it.

Bless the cheques that you write. Write 'with thanks' on them after the amount instead of 'only.' Write affirmations on the back—something like: 'Every £1 I spend blesses the recipient and returns to me multiplied.' You may get some funny looks but you could also make someone's day. The Universe will definitely respond positively.

It's common practice to be cross when a bill comes in and has to be paid. Try changing the energy! Wake up to the fact that you've been given all that power on credit; bless the bill and dance around the house in delight. How wonderful! The Electricity Company is avowing that you are prosperous enough to pay them! If they think you are, why should you disbelieve them? Even if you've automatically gone 'oh damn,' when the bill comes in, you can still turn the energy around by blessing it instead.

Many years ago I got a parking fine just before

Christmas for not reading the parking restrictions properly. As it happened, I was out somewhere where I didn't want to be which didn't help. I wasn't quite up to seeing it as a lesson in wakefulness at the time but I did know enough about the Law to know that I didn't want to pay the fine with anger and resentment because that would only bring more of the same back to me. I had a quick word with God, asking for some help and, as I was lying in the bath later on inspiration struck.

When I wrote the cheque, in the space for the amount I wrote: 'A very merry Christmas and a happy new year (oh and £25 if you really want it.)' — this is quite legal in the UK. Then I filled in the amount in numbers, signed it and picked up some felt pens to draw Christmas trees, snowmen, balloons, stars and presents all over the back and the front of the cheque. I stuck tiny metal angels wherever I found space and by the time I had finished I was laughing so much that it was a joy to post that cheque.

The fines department didn't cash it until after Twelfth Night — by which time the money to cover it had arrived totally out of the blue.

Costs

What does it actually cost for you to live every month? It is a very important practice to spend some time calculating living costs. Yes, we all wince when we realise that we have to do this — but discipline is an important part of spirituality, whether we like it or not!

Some people even leave their bills and official letters unopened or stuff them at the back of a drawer. That really is like the ostrich sticking its head in the sand. It's understandable if you have had money problems — but it sure as heck isn't going to solve them and it makes difficult situations far harder to sort out later on.

Most banks and building societies (even the

automated ones) are sympathetic if you tell them beforehand that you might have a problem. It is only afterwards that you get the worrying letters. If you are consistently overdrawn it is worth considering converting the amount into a loan—it does at least change the energy on the money. I used to have huge resistance to this when I was in debt but once I took the plunge the fact that I had a 'gentlemen's agreement' with the bank about money, rather than skulking in corners, felt a lot better. It also meant that it was a 'new debt' rather than something hanging over from my past where the energy wasn't very clear.

If it's a case of credit card bills, there are plenty of opportunities nowadays to transfer balances to new cards with lower interest rates. However, the kind of debt that chases you around is always a way of the Universe showing you that you are out of balance somewhere in your life, whether it's lack of forgiveness, holding onto the past, lack of self-worth or simply lack of attention to where your life is going. Hopefully this book will get you get clearer about what and why there may be an issue—and give you to tools to solve it.

So, what exactly is your money being used for each month?

Take a deep breath and dive into your accounts! It will take less time than you think and the satisfaction from having done it will be immense. And if you find that you have been overpaying or money is owed to you, then take time to plan a little treat for yourself to say 'thank you' for taking the time and effort to sort your finances out!

Total all your bank and credit card statements for a year and divide by twelve, for a start. It's a simple and effective way to give you a good idea. And don't think 'That was an exceptional circumstance so I'll deduct that.' There are always going to be exceptional circumstances...

Remember too, the 'hidden costs' of life which we all tend to forget and which mount up. For example, presents for birthdays and Christmas, dry cleaning bills, insurance payments, holidays, accountant's fees, pets' expenses, haircuts. Going to the movies, alcohol, cigarettes, presents for friends giving dinner parties.

And there are plenty of five-week months which make a huge difference to the outgoing bills.

When you have calculated everything, add £50 per month for incalculables and surprises and see what the total amount that you need to live comes to. You may need to stop and have a cup of tea here because it could be much more than you thought. If so, then that's the root of the prosperity problem. Take heart, it can be sorted.

Then count everything that is coming in, including presents. If there is an imbalance then start thinking about *what* you want to spend money on as opposed to what you *don't* want to spend money on. There are bound to be some things that you don't really want or need including old standing orders to 'good causes' that you no longer care about or items that represent clutter in one way or another.

Don't worry that you will need to restrict yourself. You'll find that any changes you make will have such a good knock-on effect that they will feel freeing rather than restricting. But you will need to start making positive choices over your financial affairs. Remember, every little helps. Delay a haircut for one more week. Cut out one magazine or one of the weekend newspapers. Buy a chicken, casserole it and live off it for a week instead of buying ready-made foods.

Make sure that you read your bank statements and check them off with your cheque stubs. One woman I know discovered that her mobile phone company had charged her twice for a service and she was £150 out of pocket without realising. Another realised that she had never been paid the £200 dividend she was owed on some old shares which she had had since childhood. She chased it up and found that she had earned interest on the amount, too. They certainly weren't going to chase her...

Check supermarket bills. It may sound nit-picky but it works. Sometimes the bar codes are wrong. This gives out the message that you are alert and in touch with your money.

GO TO A CASH ECONOMY

Cut back on the plastic—you cannot be in touch with your money if you can't feel it moving. Credit and debit cards are a lovely way to separate us from more money than we have because we don't feel the energy leaving at all. It is also so easy to miscalculate what you have spent unless you keep all receipts and file them.

The whole point of credit cards is to make you pay more money. The companies know full well that we all tend to think that we can afford things on a credit card when the truth is that we often can't. If you are someone who pays off the entire card at the end of each month, give yourself a pat on the back. For the rest of us it's a way of hiding our miscalculations over money whether we want to admit it or not.

If you have a credit cards and can't pay them off, get a new deal with a 0% balance transfer deal, put all your other debt onto it and take a note of the numbers (in case you need to book theatre tickets or something via the phone). *Then cut it up*. That way you can't use it on automatic when out shopping.

If you are seriously broke, go to a cash economy. It's a bit scary but effective. That, at least, teaches a short sharp lesson on where the money actually goes and shows the Universe that you are serious in your intention to change things for the better.

Exercise:

Take a £5, a £10 and a £20 note and look at them in detail so that you begin to know, recognise and understand them.

Exercise:

Work out exactly what you spend each month. You would be amazed at what slips through your fingers without your noticing it. Add £50 a month for forgotten things like haircuts, presents and breakages.

Exercise:

Change to a cash economy for a fortnight. Use cash for all your purchases and see how different it feels to handle and be in touch with money instead of avoiding it.

PERSONAL NOTES & AFFIRMATIONS

MANIFESTATION

Kick-starting Prosperity takes action; you can theorise as much as you want (and read as many books as you like) but unless you start doing the work, nothing much will happen. Affirmations are useful—they are positive statements in the present tense which inform and instruct the Universe what you want in your life. Instead of saying 'I haven't enough' try affirming 'My income is constantly increasing and I prosper wherever I turn.' It may not be true when you start but it can become true if you give it enough attention because you are re-programming your subconscious mind and putting your intention where you want your life to go.

Quantum physics has demonstrated that thought can create matter—and thought can certainly change moods and attitudes and affect the world around us. So, with positive thought and speech we strengthen certain aspects of our minds and bodies.

It's worth taking a look at what you may be attracting through unconscious actions. We've already talked about idle words creating but take a look at the pictures on the walls of your home or office.

Do they represent what you want in life—happiness, love, prosperity? If they don't, take them down right now because every time you look at them your subconscious believes that they are what you do want!

It is the nature of the human mind to make pictures for itself in your imagination—and if you don't offer it images of happy things the mind will follow the pattern set for it by whatever else it sees—whether it's what's on your wall, television, radio or in newspapers.

Once I began this work I realised that my favourite picture, which had hung above my bed for years, was of a widow looking back over happier times. I became a widow myself at the age of 33. I'm not saying I created my first husband's death but I certainly drew a man to me who was already sick when we got married. Why would the Universe think I wasn't serious when I looked at that picture so often and loved it so much?

Picturing your own prosperity is a powerful way to bring it to you and one of the best ways to do that is to create a Prosperity Wheel. This is a visual image of what you want to create which acts as a constant reminder to think about abundance and happiness instead of misery and lack.

Many spiritual teachers such as Catherine Ponder, John Assaraf or Shakti Gawain recommend Prosperity Wheels (also called Treasure Maps and Dream Boards) to help create what you need in your life.

Firstly you need to find or buy a large piece of paper or poster board, preferably coloured. Strong colours make a stronger impression on the mind. Make the wheel as big and bright and colourful as possible. Drab small images bring drab and small results!

In her book *Open Your Mind to Prosperity* (DeVorss) Catherine Ponder suggests the following colour schemes: green and gold poster boards for finances, jobs and career success. Yellow or white for spiritual understanding and development. Blue for education, intellect, writing books or articles or studying for a degree. Yellow or orange for health and energy. Pink or warm red for love, marriage, happiness in human relationships.

Once you have chosen the colour of background which best reflects your goals, find a picture of yourself looking happy and healthy and stick it in the centre of the paper. Some people prefer to put a spiritual symbol there instead of themselves but we find that the Prosperity Wheel works better with the spiritual symbol placed at the top to help channel spiritual prosperity to you.

Next work out exactly what you do want in your life, whether it's love, a new home, a car, a job, a holiday, a baby or whatever. This is vital. Prosperity wheels actually work and if you put something on one that you don't really want, you can end up with a problem.

WORDS AND PICTURES

Then find colour pictures that reflect or represent the things you want in your life and stick them on the paper around your picture. Draw lines from you to the pictures, like the spokes of a wheel, and write on them the embodiment of your dreams, such as 'I now have a loving, faithful, kind and honest partner and we love each other.' Be sure to write these 'affirmations' in the present tense. Remember how literal the Universe gets—if you want something now, you have to tell the Universe that it is already planning to send it to you.

Finally, write the all-important Universal Disclaimer on your wheel. This goes as follows:

'These things or something better now manifest for me, in easy and pleasant ways, for the highest good of all concerned.'

This is important so that you do not get the cash for that longed-for holiday through a court case or insurance after breaking a leg or you do not get anything which would hurt anyone else. You need to be very clear. Be warned that a prosperity wheel is a very powerful thing and it needs to be made and used with respect. It is vital that you ask for things for the highest good. Otherwise you are practising magic rather than spirituality and the consequences for you and others could be unpleasant.

BE CAREFUL WHAT YOU ASK FOR

Be very careful that you only ask for what you truly want. Do not go crazy and put up a picture of Russell Crowe, Jennifer Aniston or any other famous person and ask for them to be the new relationship in your life (though using their pictures to denote the type of looks that you like is okay. Just make it clear in your link to the picture that it's the *type*).

If you do want to go out with someone famous, do consider any areas of lack that desire may be revealing in you which could draw a negative rebound. Celebrity culture is a powerful force and if you did become involved with a famous person that could contribute to the the process of a costly and public divorce.

Then you might end up with stepchildren; have to move countries, the tabloids will constantly compare your face, figure and background (unflatteringly) with your predecessor who will probably bitch about you in public. You would constantly fear being replaced; you might have to live with a bodyguard watching your every move. You would never dare go out of the front door without full make-up and designer clothes (and that's just for men!) and the day after there was a huge feature on the two of you in *Hello!* magazine, you'd get dumped. Would you really want that?

What would be even worse than all that would be for you to find that you really didn't like your movie star after all and it had all been for nothing.

Just thought you'd like to know all these things.

I have drawn amazing experiences to me through prosperity wheels—and I've made a fair number of errors when making one. I asked for a sunshine holiday but put up a picture of a woman on her own... I got my holiday and, apart from the flights it was even free— but I was rather lonely during it.

Once, when I was wanting to attract love, I put up a

picture of a man looking at another woman and omitted to write 'single' on the spoke of the wheel leading to it. I attracted a man who was with another woman; who left his partner for me... and consequently left me for another woman.

My ex and I once wanted a larger home in the Midlands and we put up a picture of Gleneagles Hotel in Scotland on our dual prosperity wheel because we thought it looked lovely.

Within two weeks we had received an offer from old friends to join them in a venture of buying and restoring an old and very large house in Scotland. Rather swiftly, we took the Scottish picture down and replaced it with one of the kind of house we really wanted! We also added the words 'in the Midlands' on the spoke of the prosperity wheel leading to the house—and the perfect home turned up within months.

Another time, I started seeing herons everywhere. It was only when I realised that there was a heron in one of the holiday pictures I had put up on a wheel that I realised why. The Universe doesn't edit out *anything* on your prosperity wheel and as a heron was pretty simple for it to manifest for me, they turned up in droves.

Joanna, a woman at one of my workshops, said she desperately wanted a baby and she planned her wheel down to the last detail. But when she came to stick on the picture of the baby itself she stopped and began to cry. She had suddenly realised she was not ready for a family and that there was work to be done in the relationship with her husband before they went ahead. Without the promise of fulfilment the wheel offered her, she might not have thought the situation through and got pregnant too early.

Corinne made herself a 'family wheel' to improve relationships with her parents and brother and put a picture of herself holding her baby niece at her christening. Five months later found herself pregnant even though she was using contraception. She had put out a message to the Universe that she wanted to be holding a baby with her family's blood... so it gave her just what she had asked for.

However, the stories I know of successful and happy outcomes of prosperity wheels far outweigh the mistakes. I've seen new confidence, financial windfalls, new jobs, homes and relationships, all of which came for prosperity students who made a wheel.

Phil, who was looking for love and found it, discovered two years after his marriage that there was *actually a picture of his future wife on the wall behind the picture of him on his wheel!* Bless him, he telephoned me in America to tell me about it when he realised what had happened—and that was abundance too because we needed to clear something up between us.

Laura, who lived in a trailer in an American town, made herself a wheel—and ended up married to a rich rancher within six months. She had loved him for a long time but he had not been interested in commitment and they had split up. On her wheel, she let him go and put up a picture of another man, asking for 'her perfect committed love' to find her. As it was her former love, he came back to her and proposed.

I once made a 'love wheel' for a book proposal on prosperity and I asked a friend if I could put her picture in the centre as she was, at that time, on her own—and I had already done a wheel for myself. She said yes—and within a month she met an old friend of mine and they started going out together. The Universe saw that she wanted to find love through me—and provided it.

Usually a couple of things on your wheel will happen swiftly, as though they were only waiting your permission to manifest. Others take more time—maybe even up to a year. They can only come when your subconscious mind can accept that you deserve them, so there is often more inner work to do.

If something doesn't happen, you need to examine whether it would be for the highest good of all if it did come. If you are stuck, it is sometimes worth getting someone else's point of view on the issue.

ASK FOR YOURSELF

Do not ask for things that do not concern you. You may only represent your own desires on a prosperity wheel. It is perfectly fair to put up pictures around you of family loved ones affirming love and happiness between you because that is part of your own life. But making a prosperity wheel for someone else without their permission is interference in their life of the highest order.

If a friend or loved one is sick and you want to picture them surrounded by health and love and light, you should still get their permission first or encourage them to make a wheel for themselves. The only exceptions are if your spouse or your children are too sick to help themselves. Also, do not do a joint wheel for yourself and your partner if they are not also 100% committed to the idea with you. Otherwise they will not be contributing any energy to the outcome.

PLACEMENT

Where you place your wheel is also important. Many teachers say it should be hidden away so others cannot deride it or interfere with it. However, one woman had one of her dreams come true simply through a friend seeing what she was asking for and revealing that they knew how to achieve her goal. This one is up to you.

However, the Feng Shui of the place in your home, where the wheel is, can be important. There are areas of houses which do not have the correct flow of 'chi' to promote prosperity everywhere. If you do not know the Feng Shui of where you live, your best bet is to put the wheel next to, or on the door of, the main door into a room. This is known as 'The Gateway of Chi' and is a neutral area which will not interfere with the energies of a wheel.

Finally, look at and enjoy the pictures of what you are creating in your life. Change them as they become real or as you realise you no longer need them. When you feel you have had enough of looking at the wheel, take it down and either dismantle it or throw it away and make another one. Don't be surprised if it goes on working long after it has been taken down.

PERSONAL NOTES & AFFIRMATIONS

NEXT STEPS

PROSPERITY SUPPORT GROUPS

Prosperity Consciousness is a life's work that enhances everything within and around you. But it is best studied and undertaken with companions—just like any other spiritual work.

One of the best suggestions I can make is that you either start or find a Prosperity Support Group in your area. There are plenty of prosperity teachers who will be happy to come along to help you get going if you need them—I certainly will.

All you really need to do with such a group is to commit to meeting once a month or so and studying prosperity principles. However, you do need five or more members, otherwise it is very easy to become trapped in the same issues and situations over and over again.

You can sum up what has been happening to you over the last month; set out your aims and plans for the next month and talk about your long-term goals, giving each other support and suggestions as you go along.

Sometimes it's good to study one particular chapter of a book during the month and discuss it at the meeting with each person giving their individual responses.

Remember to open and close the group with some kind of prayer or statement of intent. This holds the energy clearly and protects you as well as others.

Other exercises you can do:

♦ Work out the perfect affirmation for each of

you and then get each person in turn to sit in the centre of a circle while you repeat that affirmation to him or her 10 times in a chorus of simultaneous voices. For example: 'Meg, you are healthy, wealthy and wise and everything you need to know is revealed to you.' This is extraordinarily moving and powerful.

♦ Pick one affirmation that you all agree on, e.g. *'The walls of lack and delay now crumble away and we enter our Promised Land under Grace'* and speak it out loud together for five minutes.

♦ Create an elimination box, a gratitudes box and a manifestation box. People can write out on Post-It notes what they want to get rid of in their life, what they are happy about and what they want to create and place them in the boxes. The elimination notes can be burnt at the end of the meeting and the others held for a month in the boxes and burnt just before the meeting. This focuses people on their goals.

You will find that the meetings organise themselves but two words of advice:

1. Have one person in charge at each meeting. This can rotate if you like but there needs to be one person who holds and directs the energy. Otherwise the meeting will become fractured or get bogged down in one particular aspect instead of being balanced.

2. Charge 'em! It is not a good idea to do this work for free. Asking for donations rather than a specific amount is fine but please make it clear that

Prosperity Consciousness is about understanding the principles of cause and effect. The time and effort of the person who hosts the meeting and the one who provides facilities for it should be recognised and honoured. You may find that a lot of people want prosperity teaching for free—but you will also discover very soon that they put no value on it and do not follow it. Putting a price on it will ensure that everyone who turns up is willing to commit to themselves and the work.

Good luck—and don't hesitate to contact me via my website **www.pureprosperity.com** or my blog www.totallylookedafter.blogspot.com with stories, ideas or questions. We are all in this together and the more we can learn and teach the better for all of us.

FURTHUR RESOURCES

Subscribers to my website www.pureprosperity.com receive a free monthly prosperity email. If you visit my blog, www.totallylookedafter.blogspot.com, you will find most of the prosperity articles from the last few years.

You can also connect with me on **www.facebook. com/maggy.whitehouse** where I host a prosperity group.

Regular prosperity support groups are running in London and Birmingham and I will happily assist you in starting up your own. Email: **mw@pureprosperity. com**.

ACKNOWLEDGEMENTS

With thanks for the inspiration, work, joy and support of:

Peter Dickinson
Gerry and Esther Hicks
Catherine Ponder
Barbara Palmer
Philip Zemke
Robin Christaens
Spuds the quarter-horse
Didcot the beagle
Bernadette Rae
Nick Williams
Jonathon Clark
Diane McDonald
Issy Benjamin

PEOPLE WHO HAVE INSPIRED YOU:

SUGGESTED READING:

The Dynamic Laws of Prosperity, Catherine Ponder (DeVorss)

Open Your Mind to Prosperity, Catherine Ponder (DeVorss)

Ask and It is Given, Jerry and Esther Hicks (Teachings of Abraham) (Hay House)

The Trick to Money, Stuart Wilde, (Rider)

The Money Bible, Stuart Wilde, (Rider)

Infinite Self, Stuart Wilde, (Hay House Inc)

The Work We Were Born to Do, Nick Williams, (Thorsons)

Unconditional Success, Nick Williams, (Thorsons)

Powerful Beyond Measure, Nick Williams, (Thorsons)

You Can Have It All, Arnold Patent (Celebration Publishing)

The Game of Life and How to Play It, Florence Scovel Shinn, (DeVorss)

The Secret Door to Success, Florence Scovel Shinn, (DeVorss)

Lessons in Truth, H. Emilie Cady, (Unity Classic)

✓ *You Can Heal Your Life*, Louise Hay, (Hay House Inc)

OTHER SOURCES OF INSPIRATION

WEBSITES

www.pureprosperity.com. Maggy's own website with prosperity tips and details of seminars, consultations and workshops.

www.abraham-hicks.com. The Abraham-Hicks partnership is one of the clearest message-givers about creating abundance that I've ever come across.

www.choosingprosperity.com—this is the American website of Elyse Hope-Killoran who also works with the Law of Attraction and which will help you work with virtual cheques for money from $100 to £1,000,000 in order to help you open your mind to prosperous thinking.

www.unityonline.org, the website of Unity Church. Don't be put off by this—Unity was founded by Charles and Myrtle Fillmore who were amazing prosperity thinkers and Unity is an open and very spiritual place based on prosperity teaching. They also have a 24-hour prayer service so, if you ever need help or support you can ask for prayers and affirmations.

www.nick-williams.com. The home of Nick Williams' *Inspired Business* website. Nick is the best at helping people to find the work they were born to do—and prosper while doing it.

www.tut.com. Mike Dooley's wonderful and inspirational site with its daily messages from the Universe.

P.40 Affirmation ②

P.41 Follow your Bliss — see list

P.47 Affirmation — ①

P.64 " short - good.

Gratitude chapter = very good

P.88 Vacuum & clutter = clear out for
" to be filled again.

P.89 Affirmations & P.90 good exercises.

P.100 - Affirmations eg; Angels of Prosperity.

* Esther & Jerry Hicks — Cards
money & the Law of Attraction.